P9-DEO-002

THE BURDEN OF THE LORD

Ian Macpherson

THE BURDEN OF THE LORD

ABINGDON PRESS
New York Nashville

THE BURDEN OF THE LORD

Library of Congress Catalog Card Number: 56-5126

SET UP, PRINTED, AND BOUND BY THE PARTHENON PRESS, AT NASHVILLE, TENNESSEE, UNITED STATES OF AMERICA

To preach the Gospel, as we have received that means of grace from our fathers, is not personal exhortation or instruction: it is a manifestation of the Incarnate Word, from the written Word, by the spoken word.

B. L. MANNING

Some people think it is such a nice, sweet, easy thing to have to do with Jesus. They read pretty stories about the Child Jesus, and the Christmas-time, and the invitation to little children, and they feel that it must be a very happy thing to be a Christ-bearer, to carry this sweet image about the world. . . . But you soon find, when the storms come, that the burden of Christ is a very, very heavy one, a serious one, which calls all your most earnest manhood into play.

P. T. FORSYTH

Contents

Chapter One

THE BURDEN

ALEXANDER GAMMIE, author and journalist, once in a newspaper article described a visit he had just paid to a fashionable Scottish church. He spoke of the storied architecture, the soul-melting music, the crowded congregation, the atmosphere of happy comradeship, the tone of workmanlike efficiency which marked the whole proceedings. And then, with that nimble pen of his, he went on to portray the preacher. "There is an air of experience about him," he wrote, "and there is certainly nothing hesitant about his manner in the pulpit. He has also an assurance which seems to carry him through a service without any sign of his being unduly oppressed by the burden of his office."

Is that seeming freedom from a burden to be reckoned unto a preacher for righteousness? Perhaps it is; for in the delivery of his message the man may have so cast himself upon God as to be rid of the care that comes of self-concern. Henry Ward Beecher referred on one occasion in a sermon to certain people who, he said, pitied him because of the heavy burden which, as a popular preacher, he was called upon to bear. "Burden!" he exclaimed. "I have no burden!" We know what he meant. To him the ministry was not a galling load, a crushing weight. It did not, in the expressive modern phrase, "get him down." And, in that sense, it doubtless *is* desirable that the preacher should not be "unduly oppressed by the burden of his office." But there is another sense—as, I think, Beecher would have been the first to agree—in which the preacher must inevitably bear a burden, a sense in which, to be sure, it is his burden that constitutes his warrant for preaching at all. Of Phillips Brooks a biographer has told that, immediately before going into the pulpit, "he appeared like one burdened with a message from God," which he was in travail to discharge. That is the proper prelude to preaching. Without it no profound and permanent impression can be made. For where there is no burden, there is no blessing.

In point of fact no fewer than four massive burdens fall to be borne by the minister of Christ. We will take them each in turn.

First, there is *the Burden of Eternity*. To many, indeed, eternity is not a burden at all: to some it is barely so much as a passing thought. Yet surely they must be very few and very blind into whose shadowed souls there do not, now and then, break "bright shoots of everlastingness"; few who have not known high hours when, with Henry Vaughan, they were fain rhapsodically to cry:

> I saw Eternity the other night,
> Like a great ring of pure and endless Light,
> All calm as it was bright.

Such lucid moods come, as I say, to all; but most people do not let them linger long in their minds. Brushing them briskly aside, they busy themselves with what they take to be the real concerns of life and so contrive, for the most part, to forget the Great Forever. Not so the true preacher. While not neglectful of the things of time, he nevertheless recognizes that, if the Christian reading of reality be right, eternity should be his prime preoccupation. On it, therefore, he broods and broods until for him it becomes a haunting burden. That is what happened, as you may remember, in the case of Bengel, the expositor. Here is his moving confession: "My greatest burden is not my weak physical frame, nor my relative afflictions, nor the attacks made on me, though from all these I have suffered. It has been hidden in my heart—the burden of eternity." No one will ever preach with power who knows nothing of that.

Again, there is *the Burden of Sinfulness.* This may, at first sight, seem strange freight for the minister of Christ to carry; yet some experience of it is the necessary precondition of strong and stirring preaching. We must be careful, of course, to distinguish clearly between the burden of sinfulness and the burden of sin. With the burden of sin the preacher, in common with the rest of men, has had perforce to reckon in the past. In the words of the poet he has had to pray:

> With my burden I begin:
> Lord, relieve my soul of sin.

Have you read Nathaniel Hawthorne's *Mosses from an Old Manse,* and do you recollect that vivid and arresting scene where, rummaging about among the virtuoso's collection, he stumbled over a big bundle, like a peddler's pack, wrapped up in sackcloth and tightly strapped and corded? "It is the Christian's burden of sin," explains the virtuoso.

"Oh, pray, let me see it," begs the other. "For many a long year I have yearned to know its contents."

"Look into your own conscience and memory," comes the reply. "You will find there a list of whatever it contains." That is the burden of sin. But this is different. This is the burden of sinfulness. The burden of sin is something which, on certain terms, Christ lifts from men: the burden of sinfulness is something which Christ lays upon men—that leaden load which caused the holy Lancelot Andrewes to confess, "I am made of sin"; and William Law, devout and saintly man though he was, to call himself "a dead dog"; and Alexander Whyte, one of the rarest souls God ever gave to Scotland, to refer to himself as "the worst man in Edinburgh."

Such expressions of extreme self-contempt are not to be lightly dismissed as mere pious hyperbole, the maudlin exaggerations of morbidly introspective minds. They are the words of honest men, and we must take them as they stand. That was really how those ripe saints felt about themselves, and the fact that they did so was no small part of the secret of their pulpit power. "In my younger days," remarks Richard Baxter, "my concern was most about my actual thought, word, or action. But now I am much more troubled for the inward defects and omissions, or want of vital virtues or graces in the soul. These are the greatest burden of my life."

Once more, there is *the Burden of Souls*. Here you have a further bundle for the preacher's back. Of him it will be characteristic that, like Wesley, he will have "a great concern for folk," not alone for those specifically committed to his care—though they will, of course, have first call on his attention!—but also for all whose need gives them a claim upon him. Recognizing that all who perish are in his parish, he will want to do whatever he can toward their reclamation and recovery. For the highest welfare of each he will feel a personal and particular responsibility, as one who must give account.

Consider how nobly some of the notable preachers of the past did that. "My witness is above," declared Samuel Rutherford, "that your heaven would be two heavens to me, and the salvation of you all as two salvations to me. I would agree to a suspension and postponement of my heaven for many hundreds of years, if ye could so be assured of a lodging in the Father's house." Of John Welch it is told that he would spend long hours on his knees by his bedside, even on winter nights, praying and weeping in the darkness, with only his plaid flung about his shoulders to shield him from the cold, and that his wife, poor creature, would expostulate with him and bid him return to his rest, only to receive the reply: "Oh, woman, I have the souls of three thousand to answer for, and I know not how it is with many of them." John Bunyan, for his part, as you may recall, actually went so far as to say that he would sooner follow one of his natural children, begotten of his own body, to the grave than lose one of the spiritual children God had given him. Such are some challenging and inspiring examples of this pastoral passion for souls. Wanting it, no man will ever make much of a minister.

But, while it belongs to the preacher's sacred office to bear each of the burdens of which I have spoken, there is one burden which, before all others, it is his special business and privilege to carry and without which he is disqualified from preaching altogether.

"To the natural man," says T. S. Taylor, "the burden of preaching consists in listening to it, and there can be no doubt about his increasing tendency to rid himself of that burden." That may be so; and yet it is indubitable that the more preaching is a burden, in the one sense, to the preacher, the less will it be a burden, in the other sense, to the hearers. At all events it is most certainly the distinctive and inalienable duty of the minister of Christ to be the bearer of a burden, and that burden the *Burden of the Lord.*

Why this is so will appear as we proceed to examine the nature and function of Christian preaching. For what, after all, *is* Christian preaching? Notice in what terms the New Testament normally and most characteristically refers to the nature and substance of Christian preaching. It does not speak about preaching religion; it does not speak about preaching Christianity; surprisingly enough, it does not speak nearly as often as we should have expected about preaching the gospel. About what, then, does it speak? It speaks about preaching Christ!

Were evidence required, it could be adduced in abundance. Is it of the preaching of Peter and the rest of the apostles that it is telling? Here is what it says: "They ceased not to teach and preach Jesus Christ." Is it of the ministry of Philip, the evangelist, it is making mention? Here is how it does so: "Then Philip went down to the city of Samaria, and preached Christ unto them." Is it to the message of Saul of Tarsus, suddenly and dramatically converted on the road to Damascus, that it is attracting attention? Here is the record as it sets it down: "Straightway he preached Christ in the synagogues."

It cannot too strongly be stressed that the definitive content of the earliest Christian preaching was not a set of ethical rules or a philosophical theory or a social program: it was not even, in the last resort, a series of phenomenal events—though it did herald the most astounding happenings! The distinctive content of the earliest Christian preaching may be summed up in one word—*Christ!*

"Preaching Christ." That is a pregnant phrase. There is more in it than meets the casual eye. It is not to be equated with mere preaching *about* Christ. You can preach about Confucius or Socrates or the Buddha or Mohammed, and you can preach about Christ too. But that is not preaching in the New Testament sense. Preaching, in the New Testament sense, is, as we have seen, not preaching about Christ but preaching Christ himself, and you cannot so preach Confucius or Socrates or the Buddha or Mohammed.

Christian preaching, therefore, is not the bare utterance of words, however skillfully woven on the loom of literary or oratorical art: it is infinitely more—the communication of *the* Word, the bearing and the delivery of a burden and that burden the Burden of the Lord, not just the burden which the Lord bestows, but the Burden which the Lord himself is! Hence preaching is something august, sublime, awe-begetting—a supernatural act, the transmission *of* a Person *through* a person *to* a company of persons, the Person so conveyed being the everlasting Jesus.

Every true sermon is a Bethlehem. Above it the star sparkles and about it shimmer troops of shouting angels. Hearing it, wise men bring their gifts and bow themselves, and the world is made glad by the coming of its Saviour. As really as Christ was historically mediated to mankind through the body of Mary, "when the humble Hebrew maiden became the mother of her God," so really is Christ mystically mediated to mankind through a true preacher.

It is no mere curiosity of language that the noun used in the Latin version of the New Testament to translate the Greek *logos* in the opening verses of John's Gospel is *sermo*—a term from which our English word "sermon" is directly derived. To feel the full force of this striking fact it is necessary to study the Prologue to the Fourth Gospel in the light of it, putting the term "sermon" in the place of "Word" wherever it occurs. Listen: "In the beginning was the Sermon, and the Sermon was with God, and the Sermon was God." Dare anyone say that about his pulpit prelections? Can any preacher rationally claim that his ministerial deliverances are to be construed under so colossal a category? It may seem daring and presumptuous to suggest it, but in so far as his utterances are genuinely inspired and not defective or distorted through his human liability to error, he may justly make for them that stupendous claim.

Campbell Morgan, in his valuable little volume *Preaching*, significantly reminds us that there is really no warrant for the distinction drawn in our English Bibles between the term "Word" when spelled with a capital "W" and when spelled with a small "w." Nothing in the original corresponds to that distinction. Think, then, what this implies. Perhaps it can best be brought out by setting two typical quotations side by side. First this: "And the Word was made flesh, and dwelt among us." And then this: "And they . . . went every where preaching the word." You will notice that, in the former case, the translators have used a capital "W" and in the latter a small "w." Why? Probably they were actuated by what they felt to be the fitness of things. But were they right? By no means, for the procedure is without the slightest support in the original. In both contexts it is the same Word.

The importance of this for the study of preaching is obvious. It regulates and reorientates the whole subject. For, if this be fact, it follows that preaching is not the feeble thing for which all too frequently it passes but a tremendous thing—nothing less than the communication through the utterance of a consecrated personality of the eternal Christ.

Is it not precisely thus that the great preachers of history have interpreted their huge task? "Were the highest heavens my pulpit," cried an ancient Church father, "and the whole host of the redeemed my audience, Jesus alone would be my text." "We preach always Christ, and Christ alone, true God and true man," exclaimed Martin Luther; "that may seem a limited and monotonous subject, likely to be soon exhausted, but we are never at the end of it." "I have tried to preach Jesus Christ," claimed Alexander Maclaren, reviewing the strenuous years of his mighty ministry in Manchester, "the Jesus Christ, not of the Gospels only, but the Christ of the Gospels and the Epistles." Manifestly these eminent ministers conceived themselves to be, beyond all else, bearers of the Burden of the Lord.

Be quite clear, then, as prospective preachers, where your primary duty lies. It does not lie in the dissection of dead dogma, nor in the spinning of superfine theological speculations, nor in the organization of a social group, nor in the elucidation of political and economic problems. Your primary duty lies here: you are to be bearers of the Burden of the Lord. You are to carry Christ to the people. Through you, as through Mary of old, God is to come omnipotently into his world.

To say that is not to imply anything merely automatic or mechanical in the process. The preacher's personality is not to be thought of as no more than a kind of conduit by means of which the Word is conveyed like water through a pipe: rather may he be likened to the trunk of a living tree with the sap seeping through every fiber. When the Word was born of Mary, he did not, so to speak, transmit himself magically, without partaking of her nature or assimilating her substance. On the contrary, he laid hold of her very flesh and blood, brought into vital concentrated action every part of her dedicated being. So with the minister and his message. When, in true preaching, the Word is livingly communicated, the personality of the preacher is not dormant or passive. Far from it. Only when his every power and faculty are brought into full, harmonious, and vigorous display can the Word be properly conveyed at all.

Preaching, we have said, is above all the conveyance *of* a Person *through* a person *to* a company of persons, the Person so conveyed being the Lord Jesus Christ. Well, if that be so, one thing inevitably follows: he who really preaches is bound to have a big theme! Never forget that the Holy Spirit does not visit with lubricating unction the soul of the preacher who deals in homiletical drivel, but only that of him who gets to grips with the great redemptive realities. Gossip speaks witheringly somewhere about certain preachers "pirouetting," as he picturesquely puts it, "with some pretty bit of a text on the outskirts of things." That is tragic folly and I trust you will never be justly chargeable with it. Do not in your sermons, I beseech you, nibble away at niceties in the sacred text, nor balance your discourses precariously on the tips of their biblical toes. Have the good sense to realize that it is hardly likely that the Almighty will have made eternal salvation to turn on a Hebrew point or a Greek particle. "Be not nice" was Wesley's curt counsel to his preachers. Avoid a prim and mincing ministry. Shun pedantry like the plague. Paint on a large canvas. You are to be in the pulpit to do tremendous work. Wherefore focus all your forces on the central task. Concentrate massively on the main thing. Preach Christ!

At this juncture, though, we run up against a practical difficulty. It is to deal greatly with the great theme. How dreadfully easy it is to dwarf a big subject by treating it inadequately! You do your best, of course, but the thing just falls to bits in your hands. Could there be a more damning indictment of a preacher than this from the mordant pen of W. R. Maltby: "He spoke of great things and made them small, of holy things and made them common, of God and made Him of no account"? It is vital that, to the very limit of his powers, the preacher shall deal greatly with the great theme.

Perhaps the classical example of this deporable cheapening of the focal truths of Christianity is furnished by the following quotation from the writings of a famous Dutch historian. He is describing preaching in Germany during the second half of the eighteenth century, and he has this to say:

> Who has not of the Christmas sermon on the stall-feeding of cattle, of the Epiphany sermon on listening to good counsels, of the Palm Sunday sermon on the damaging of trees, of the Easter sermon on the benefits of a walk (the travellers to Emmaus), the Pentecost sermon on drunkenness, and so on?

That is the pulpit at its worst, treating sublime topics trivially, making the magnificent look mean.

Few ministers of the Word today are in danger of descending to such depths. Most err perhaps in the opposite direction, shrinking from handling the large issues lest they shrivel at their touch. That, however, is also a profound mistake. "A man," as Maclaren maintains, "should begin early to grapple with great subjects. As the athlete gains by great exertions, so a man does not overstrain his powers by taking great texts. The more he wrestles, the more he will gain strength." Nevertheless, apart from such personal advantages accruing from thus dealing with the central theme, you would do well ever to keep before you the fact that, as preachers and therefore by definition bearers of the Burden of the Lord, you are certain always to have a colossal subject and that it is your bounden duty to deal with it as worthily as you can.

Do not, however, deduce from this that you are to strive to preach what are commonly styled "great" sermons. That would be a false inference. Never try to be great: the very effort will make you small. Greatness, if it is to come your way at all, will come without your being aware of it. May I remind you of that singular petition in the old Moravian liturgy, "From the unhappy desire of becoming great, good Lord, deliver me"? Make that your daily prayer, if you are prone to preen yourself on your prowess as a preacher; for remember that while the weathercock is traditionally entitled to a place on the spire of the church, the peacock is entirely out of place in its pulpit!

"Every young man who is aspiring," wrote Henry Ward Beecher, "wants to do great things and to preach great sermons. Great sermons ninety-nine times in a hundred are great nuisances." Without going all the way with him there—and in any case he probably did not *mean* us to go all the way with him, for he himself preached great sermons!—we may as well confess that there is considerable truth in what he says. At the same time, if a man grapple with the great theme, for all his thumby handling of it, something of the sublimity of the subject may insensibly communicate itself to the sermon. Yet do not set out with the deliberate design of preaching super-sermons, or you are like to defeat your own object, since the best sermons are never merely ends in themselves but are always composed with a view to something beyond themselves.

Nor, again, does the fact that you are to preach Christ imply that you are to attempt to cram into one fat discourse a whole compendium of Christian doctrine. Christ may be viewed from an infinite variety of angles and portrayed in a multiplicity of aspects. Do not suppose that you can possibly put all there is to say about him into one obese sermon, and do not try to do so. Just as Mont Blanc—"the Great White Throne," as Frances Ridley Havergal strikingly called it—appears kaleidoscopically different when glimpsed from various Alpine vantage points, so Christ looks different, in some sense, to a developing Christian every day. (Not that he really changes, but that our sense of the sheer wonder of him grows!) No sermon can do more than catch and reflect a single facet of his variegated glory. Besides, looking at the matter from the angle of common prudence, is it not desperately bad policy to stuff into one stout address all your little stock of thought? Better heed the sententious counsel of William Taylor of New York: "Keep something for again."

Your business, then, is to preach Christ. He is to be the Burden of your ministry. But *how* are you to preach him? I offer three suggestions. First, *Preach Christ evangelically, as Saviour and Lord;* second, *Preach Christ ethically, as Teacher and Example;* third, *Preach Christ eschatologically, as destined Judge and Ruler of the world.*

I

Preach Christ evangelically, as Saviour and Lord. Begin there. Let that be the first plank in your platform. But what does it involve? Surely three things: one, that you present Christ as an eternal Being; two, that you depict him as a historical Figure; three, that you portray him as a contemporary Power.

Begin by presenting Christ as an eternal Being. This is inevitable. Any adequate Christology necessarily implies a doctrine of the Trinity, since you cannot satisfactorily account for that extraordinary Character, Jesus of Nazareth, save as you regard his life on earth as the extension in time of the existence in eternity of the august and awful One whom we designate the second Person in the Godhead. At the mention of the Trinity some may be tempted to demur, protesting that a theme so abstract and abstruse is scarcely suitable for popular treatment in the pulpit. I readily admit that in the hands of a clumsy and unimaginative preacher such a subject could all too easily become dull and tedious to a degree. Yet surely it need not do so. Everything depends on how you handle it.

Of course, if you begin by making an excursion into remote Church history and revive the terminology of the Athanasian controversy when, as Carlyle, following Gibbon, contemptuously expressed it, the world was divided over a diphthong (though he came later to see that the diphthong was immeasurably important!), or if you soar into the cloudy realm of metaphysics and dilate at learned length on academic abstractions, you are likely to be greeted, as you deserve to be, with the inattention of indifference.

But suppose you set about things otherwise. Suppose you begin by pointing out that the basic pattern in human society is threefold —father, mother, child—and then suppose you proceed to contend that this fundamental social design finds its original in the Godhead, that this is in fact the structure, if one may so speak, of the eternal Trinity—God the Father, God the Mother (the Holy Spirit), and God the Son. There is a striking uncanonical saying attributed to Christ which has the ring of reality about it and which you may quote in this connection: "My Mother, the Holy Ghost."

But in truth you need not travel so far in pursuit of evidence that the Holy Spirit is the feminine principle in the Trinity and that the Godhead may thus properly be spoken of as a Family, for the Bible itself is full of it. Preaching in this way, you will not be talking about some vague trinitarian formula, the fossilized expression of an antique faith: you will be talking about something with which your hearers will all be thoroughly familiar—a Family. And in the midst of that Family you will picture One like unto the Son of God. Present Christ, then, as an eternal Being.

But, further, depict him also as a historical Figure. Yes, but how? First, report certain facts concerning him; next, propound a theological interpretation of those facts; and, then, demonstrate the practical relevance of the facts to life as we know it today.

Begin with the fact of *a Baby in a cradle*. About that there is a homely actuality. A Baby in a cradle! Whatever mystery may lie at the heart of our holy faith—and, mark you, it could not be a faith at all unless it contained some element of mystery!—here at any rate we are in the region of concrete reality. Here is the solid stuff of history. Here is an elemental human fact—a Baby in a cradle! And it is with that human fact that you have first of all to deal in your evangelical presentation of Christ.

Beyond the fact, however, lies the interpretation of the fact. What are you to make of that? In all honesty it must be owned that some do not make very much of it. They see in it little more than an addition to the population of ancient Palestine, another name to be set down on the census roll of Augustus Caesar, the emergence of a great religious Teacher, and so on. But in your interpretation of this tremendous incident you will have to go much further. You will have to assert with all possible emphasis that this newborn Babe was the everlasting God come down, that this Infant "with no language but a cry" was the eternal Word that spoke the worlds out of the womb of nothing, that the tiny arms of this helpless Child were the limbs of him who laid the timbers of the universe.

Some of your hearers will, by the grace of God, assent to that; some will not. A proportion of those listening to you will accept it with adoring wonder; others will summarily reject it as a mere piece of sentimental rhapsodizing, a pretty fantasy fathered by the pious fancy. But, whether men hear or whether they forbear, such is the construction which in your preaching you must ever place on the historic fact of the coming of Christ.

Yet do not leave off there. Proceed to proclaim the pertinence of the Incarnation at the present hour. Show its imperial relevance now. In these days when so many speculations are abroad respecting the nature of the Being behind all being; when some, like Bernard Shaw, are declaring that it is a soulless Force, and some, with Bertrand Russell, that it is a blind Fate, and some, like H. G. Wells in a wild mood, that it is a malignant Foe—in these days, I say, and in this predominantly secular age, no article of Christian belief is more practically to the point than the great doctrine of the Incarnation. For that doctrine affirms that behind the phenomena of the visible world there is neither a mere Force nor a mindless Fate nor a malicious Foe, but a loving Father; it affirms that the unseen Being at the back of things displayed his essential character by begetting a Son, and that that Son perfectly reveals him.

Among the thousands thronging Trafalgar Square in London every day some doubtless look up in passing at the statue of Lord Nelson on top of its colossal column and try to make out what it is really like. The effort is not easy. In his well-meaning concern to give the famous admiral as exalted a position as possible the sculptor has set him too high to be distinctly discernible from the pavement below. The elevation precludes revelation. At an exhibition in 1948, however, an exact replica in plaster of the figure surmounting the tremendous pillar was placed at eye level, where all could closely examine it. Thus for the first time many had an immediate view of the features which before they had only beheld from afar. That is what Jesus did for God. He brought him down, if one may so say, to our level, within range of our dimly finite vision, so that we might see him face to face. At Bethlehem the Most High became the most nigh. "And the Word was made flesh, and dwelt among us, and we beheld his glory."

That is the first fact with which in your evangelical preaching you will have to get to grips—the fact of a Baby in a cradle who is also the Lord God Almighty.

The second is the fact of *a Man on a cross*. Once more we are in the theater of historic actuality. A Man on a cross! Not an ivory image on an ebony crucifix, but a real live human being lifted up in agony upon two rough logs. There is a second fact for you.

What is the import of it? We do well to ask that, for it is its import that gives it its importance. Many men have hung upon crosses. In those crude and cruel days crucifixion was a popular mode of punishment and the spectacle of a blood-drenched corpse hanging blackening in the sun on a couple of beams by the common highway was a sight so familiar that few wayfarers so much as bothered to turn their heads and look at it. What is there about this Man to differentiate him from all others and to mark him out for special notice? Clearly it all depends upon who you think he was and upon what you think he was dying for. Well, who *was* he and what was the nature of his death? There are various views. One says that he was a martyr dying for his principles, and that his cross is to be placed in the same category as the hemlock that poisoned Socrates and the faggots that burned John Hus and the bullet that cut short the life of Abraham Lincoln. Another says that he was a patriot dying for his country and that his death deserves to rank along with those of Judas Maccabeus and Joan of Arc and William Wallace. But in your interpretation of the fact of the cross you will have to go far beyond that. You will have to declare that he was a Saviour dying for the world!

In Dora Greenwell's *Life of Lacordaire* there is a grimly memorable passage in which, describing with graphic realism the fanatical austerities to which the famous preacher subjected himself as a mode of moral discipline, she tells how, one Good Friday, he descended with a single companion into the crypt of an ancient church in Paris and there, in the eerie half-darkness, among long rows of low vaults filled with bones and death's-heads, came upon two dusty beams which he hammered together in the form of a cross and, laying his body upon the boards, had himself bound upon them hand and foot, remaining thus for three hours.

How different was the crucifixion of Christ! Lacordaire, as he appeared on that occasion, was a man dying in make-believe for himself: upon the cross Jesus was, on the contrary, a Man dying in reality for the whole world.

That the world desperately needed dying for is appallingly apparent. Plainly there is something radically wrong with it, a fundamental disharmony, an elemental dislocation, a basic bias toward evil. You can try to account for the fact of sin as you like. You can call it a theological fiction, a pathological state deliberately fomented in the public mind by the salaried representatives of religion with a view to implementing their own ends and securing their own vested interests. You can call it an evolutionary legacy, the moral hangover from our alleged animal ancestry. You can call it "good in the making," "the growing pains of the race," or what you will. The one thing you cannot do is to deny that it has made havoc of God's fair earth. Scripture declares that the havoc is so dreadful that even an omnipotent God could only save the world by dying for it! Such is the interpretation which as preachers you are to offer of the historic fact of the cross.

What of its practical relevance? That, surely, is clear. He who died for the world died for everyone in it. The universal includes the unit. The cosmic comprehends the individual. This is well. For sin is not simply a social or ethnic phenomenon: it is something intensely personal. The world within is as warped as the world without, and what is salvation but the thrilling discovery that Christ died for that world no less than for the other? Such, at any rate, is to be your application of the great truth of the Atonement.

A Man on a cross! There is the second huge fact which, in your evangelical preaching of Christ, you will require to handle.

The third is the fact of *a Body in a tomb*. Here, again, we are in the domain of definite objective reality. A Body in a tomb! The historicity of the entombment of Christ has never seriously been called in question. Every detail of the poignant and dramatic scene stands out before us with stark and clear-cut vividness as we scan the sacred documents. The cave, carved in the living rock; the corpse lying cold on a ledge within; the circular stone rolled to the mouth of the sepulcher, bearing the imperial seal; the Roman guards posted nearby, those nervous nights, the moonlight flashing from their helmets and spears—we see it all as plainly as if we had been there in person and had witnessed it for ourselves. A Body in a tomb! There is a further fact for you. But really it is only half of the fact. The other half is that on the third day after burial the Body was in the tomb no longer! What had happened? Opinion is divided. Some allege that Jesus did not really die on the cross at all, that he only swooned, and that when his body was deposited in the grave in Joseph's garden, the cool atmosphere of the cavern and the pungent perfumes of the aromatic spices stung him back to consciousness; and that eventually he was able to muster enough strength to struggle to his feet, strip off the encumbering shroud and stagger forth into the light of dawn. But manifestly this theory is utterly untenable. To refute it, it is only necessary to remember how the spear of a Roman soldier stabbed in wanton brutality into the body of the dead Redeemer provides surgical evidence that he really did die; and, in any case, it is impossible not to agree here with Strauss when he contends that a pale and bloodless Christ, in urgent need of hospital treatment, dragging himself slowly and painfully from the sepulcher would hardly have been likely to persuade his followers, as Jesus actually did persuade them, that he had triumphed over the tomb. Others maintain that it was not the real body of Christ that rose from the grave on that momentous morning but only a ghost that floated forth, a thin impalpable wraith, a sort of ectoplasmic emanation. But, as W. A. Kirkland convincingly argues in her excitingly eloquent book *Who Is This Jesus?*:

> It is a new thing in ghost stories which turns abject terror into flaming courage and cowards into heroes and martyrs. It drove ordinary, shrinking men, like ourselves, to go shouting a message to audiences as derisive as some men are today, a message punished with stripes and crosses and red-jowled beasts, yet persisting, indomitable, on and on, down the echoing centuries, until a pagan world was conquered by a handful of Jewish fishermen and a great Church raised its pinnacles to heaven to enshrine that message flung to the wind on Easter Sunday.

It takes more than a ghost to account for Christian history. No ghost but the Holy Ghost could have brought about the mighty changes which have been wrought in human society since that dramatic dawn, and *he* assures us that Jesus is alive and that the glorious revolution is to be set down as the personal, post-mortem achievement of the Son of God. Yet another theory is that Jesus did not really rise from the dead, but that his disciples—poor, deluded, neurotic, uncritical, impressionable folk!—only fancied that he had. But were the followers of Christ in the frame of mind thus to be taken in? Were their imaginations heated by religious hysteria? Had they worked themselves up into the mood that hatches such hallucinations? Not at all. The plain truth is that they were not the type of people who are prone to such imaginings and that, in any case, their mental condition at the time was the very opposite of that which this theory presupposes. So far from being full of excited anticipation, they were dully unexpectant, struck dumb by a sudden stunning sorrow. Would such men in such a state be likely to see such an apparition as they are said to have seen, and to have seen it not once only, but in different places and at different times? No! The supposition puts too severe a strain on our credulity. We dismiss it as undeserving of serious consideration. Yet another contention is that the sepulcher of Christ was empty because his enemies came by night and stole him away. But, if that were so, why did they not produce the body or indicate its whereabouts when, a day or two later, rumors that Jesus had risen were running through the city like fire through dry heather? The natural assumption is that they *did not* produce the body because they *could not* produce the body. It had never been in their possession. One last theory remains. This is that not Christ's foes but his friends rifled the tomb and removed the corpse. But this notion also can easily be disposed of. How could the disciples, weak and cowardly as they had proved themselves to be, have overpowered the Roman guards and broken Caesar's seal? Besides—a weightier difficulty by far!—were they the sort of people to do such a thing and then to foist upon mankind a wicked fraud and *die* for it, to boot! We cannot credit it. It is easier to believe in the Resurrection than to believe that. And it is that fact of the Resurrection to which you are to bear ringing witness in your evangelical presentment of Christ.

But what of the interpretation? It may be construed in various ways. You may speak of it as the vindication of the values for which Christ stood, as the signal of divine approval on the work of redemption, as the pledge and prophecy of our human conquest of death. However you contemplate it, you are bound to confess that it is a titanic fact. If this is not true, then it does not ultimately matter very much what is true; if this never happened, then it were just as well that nothing should ever have happened; if this is but illusion, then God himself stands convicted for having created beings who, like Shakespeare's Cleopatra, have immortal longings in them, and yet denied them the immortality for which they crave. Were you to blot out this tremendous happening and all its implications from the calendar, it would be like repeating the process of creation in reverse—striking the sun from the heavens and leaving only a vast void and darkness upon the face of the deep. That is the construction which, in your evangelical preaching, you are to put upon the colossal fact of the resurrection of Christ.

To inquire whether such a fact is relevant to the situation today were in truth superfluous. Nothing could conceivably be more so.

Right in the heart of London, in the Egyptological section of the British Museum, there is a stone coffin containing the body of a man who died three thousand years ago. The body has been marvelously preserved by the dry sand in which it was buried and which has indeed crudely embalmed it, so that the whole form is still intact after thirty centuries—the skin, like old sallow parchment, covering the framework of bone. The figure is in a crouching position and resembles a large question mark. And sometimes as I have looked down upon it and reflected that round it, as it lies there, revolves the mightiest city of the modern world, a humming hive of human activity, I have felt that that mummy is a sort of ironical comment on it all, a grim mark of interrogation, symbolizing, as it were, the immemorial question of the patriarch Job: "If a man die, shall he live again?"

The question is timelessly relevant. All the bafflement and tragedy of life, its haunting mysteries, its blanching sorrows, its paralyzing frustrations, are bound up with that. If there is no affirmation in response to that poignant point of interrogation, then there is no meaning anywhere. All the lamps of life have gone out and we are left forever in the dark. "But now is Christ risen from the dead!" *There* is the clue to your riddle, the healing of your hurt, the promise of the final fulfillment of your highest hopes and noblest aspirations.

A Body in a tomb? No! not that, but Christ risen in power and great glory is the third fact with which, as evangelical preachers, you will have to grapple.

The fourth fact is that of *a King on a throne*. Is it not eminently noteworthy that, alike at the beginning and at the end of his earthly life, Jesus was proclaimed King? At his birth, wise men came from the east, inquiring: "Where is he that is born King of the Jews?"—and at his death Pilate nailed to the beam above his head a board with the inscription: "This is Jesus the King of the Jews." Moreover, twice in the crowded interval between, Christ was offered a crown—once by Satan during the temptation in the wilderness and once by the people when, swept off their feet by the magnetism of his manhood and the magnificence of his achievements, they sought to make a monarch of him by main force. But, if his innate royalty was thus splendidly apparent even in the days of his flesh, when he was subject to the limitations incident to the Incarnation, how much more manifest was it when, having laid those inhibiting restrictions aside, he ascended into heaven and sat down on the right hand of the Majesty on high? A King on a throne! There is a fourth fact for you.

How are you to interpret it? Once again there are various possibilities. You may talk of it as the personal triumph of Christ, or you may refer to it as illustrating the supremacy of spiritual values, or you may take it as a token of the perfectibility of human nature. At all events do not fail to proclaim it with fearless and impassioned forthrightness. In this ambiguous world the final issue of the moral conflict is not in doubt. Christ is not struggling to the seat of power. He is already on the throne!

That such a fact is thrillingly pertinent to our present needs is perfectly plain. What could be more bracing and nerving and rallying and exhilarating than the spectacle of a *Man* on the throne? Depressed, as we all are at times, by the daunting difficulties of the moral life, discouraged and distressed by the absence of perceptible progress in our own characters, we are often almost tempted to doubt our own ultimate redeemability and to question whether we ever shall be perfect as our Father in heaven is perfect. But when we see a *Man* on the eternal throne, we take heart of grace. His coronation is the pledge and prophecy of the possibility of ours.

Thus, by stressing four great facts—that of *a Baby in a cradle, a Man on a cross, a Body in a tomb,* and *a King on a throne*—you will preach Christ stirringly as a historical Figure.

But you will not stop there. *You will portray him also as a contemporary Power.* And this calls for a personal encounter on your part with the dynamic of Pentecost. To some men Jesus is no more than a prisoner of the past, a character in a book, a memory blown to us across a widening waste of years; not to say, a pathetic little pile of powdered bone, a handful of phosphorus amid the dust of a forgotten grave. To others he is a vision disappearing up the sky, a Christ in retreat, vanishing into vacuity. Such a Christ could be of interest only to archaeologists or to mystics. But Pentecost brings the gripping assurance that Christ is not in retreat but gloriously on the advance, not melting into the distance but moving with might into our immediate circumstances. It is not enough to see Christ going away, even if you know he is going to a throne: you must also see him coming with power. And to see him coming with power you will have to experience that vitalizing invasion, that rush of supernatural energy, that came to the first disciples in the Upper Room. Pentecost makes Christ our great Contemporary, takes him out of the mists of antiquity into the swirl and sweep of current events, gives him hands to grapple with the urgent issues of the present hour.

Yet more: it causes him to be the radiating focus of a world-wide fellowship. Every great institution centers in some dominating personality. The United States of America finds its principle of cohesion in the presidency; the British Commonwealth of nations is integrated by its loyalty to the crown. But there is an institution more wonderful by far than any federation of states or community of peoples. It is the Church of the living God. And what is the personality which forms its organizing focus? It is not the pope, for the papacy is not as catholic as it professes to be. It is no ecclesiastical dignitary, however eminent; no religious potentate, however influential. It is the risen Christ himself. He is the center of that fellowship, alike in the cosmic as in the congregational sense. The whole Christian communion on earth and in heaven and the smallest company that assembles in his name find their force of gravitation in the magnetism of the unseen Master. At the heart of both stands the risen Redeemer. You will preach Christ evangelically, as Saviour and Lord.

II

You will preach him, too, ethically, as Teacher and Example. A false antithesis has sometimes been instituted between evangelical and ethical preaching. It has been supposed that the two are incompatible or even mutually exclusive. On the one hand, it has been complained that evangelical preachers seem to have ignored the ethical realities, propounding their distinctive doctrines in detachment from the moral issues of life. On the other hand, some have protested, not without reason, against the tendency of certain preachers to treat the New Testament as little more than a textbook on etiquette at the court of heaven and to reduce the robust religion of Jesus to a bare code of conduct, making it a mere matter of doing the decent thing, practicing the common commercial virtues, and so forth.

Against the first of these errors John Foster inveighed at the beginning of the nineteenth century:

> In the department of Christian morality I think many of those who are distinguished as evangelical preachers are greatly and culpably deficient. They rarely, if ever, take some one topic of moral duty as honesty, veracity, impartiality, temper, forgiveness of injuries, the improvement of time, and investigate specifically its principles, rules, discriminations, adaptations. Such discussions would cost far more labour than dwelling and

expatiating on the general evangelical doctrines, but would have been eminently useful.

As to the second of the errors the charge has often been laid against Tillotson and other preachers of that school that they enforced Christian duty far oftener than they expounded Christian doctrine, and that thus they caused Christianity to appear more as demand than as offer, more as good advice than as good news.

Where, then, in this debate does the truth really lie? It lies, as so frequently it does in such cases, between the two extremes. So far from being contradictory, the two forms of preaching are actually complementary, and the Christ who is preached as Saviour and Lord must also be set forth as Teacher and Example. An unevangelical ethicalism is cold, formal, lacking in moral drive: an unethical evangelicalism is fanatical, sentimental, unpractical. We need both. They are the two wings of a bird, the two oars of a boat, the two hands of a clock. Each is essential as the counterpart of the other.

There is no finer way of inculcating in your people the principles of Christian ethics than by proclaiming the great evangelical facts. Thomas Chalmers, you may recollect, found that. In his farewell discourse to his flock at Kilmany he declared: "You have at least taught me that to preach Christ is the only effective way of preaching morality in all its branches." And David Brainerd, among the redskins of North America, registered the same discovery. "I find," he recorded, "that my Indians begin to put on the garments of holiness, and their common life begins to be sanctified even in a trifle, when they are possessed by the doctrine of Christ and Him crucified."

> Talk they of morality, O Thou bleeding Lamb:
> The true morality is love of Thee.

Conversely, it is immensely significant that many of the leading figures in the history of evangelicalism have owed their conversions under God to the preaching of ethical sermons. To this Alexander Whyte bears impressive testimony:

> The Apostle Paul, next to Jesus Christ, is our greatest possession, and we owe the apostle to a sermon on the Tenth Commandment. And we owe St Augustine, our next possession after St Paul, to a sermon on the Seventh Commandment. And we owe John Bunyan—and you all know what a possession he is—to a sermon on the Fourth Commandment, and Samuel Johnson to a sermon on the same commandment and to another on the Fifth Commandment.

Neither type of preaching, therefore, excludes the other. Both are necessary. Side by side with your presentation of Christ as Saviour and Lord you will protray him as Teacher and Example.

Never was the world more urgently in need of an adequate ethical ideal. Morals are in the melting pot. Behavior has become the subject of experiment. Standards of conduct which for centuries have been regarded as sacrosanct in all civilized countries are now, in the name of a false freedom, being challenged and flouted and flung to the winds. Pagan gods are being erected in the temple of fame, and the youth of today is bowing down to them with calamitous consequences. Desperately we require a worthy moral ideal.

Where shall we find it? I submit that among all the claimants for the world's moral leadership in these days there is none who is fit to hold a candle to Jesus of Nazareth. Alone, on the very farthest verge and frontier of ethical achievement, he stands without a peer. None but he perfectly exhibits in his character the qualities which he extols in his teaching. All others fall short somewhere. No one commends chastity more forthrightly than does Shakespeare in a famous passage in *The Tempest*: yet Shakespeare himself "had," as we say, "to be married." Howard, the humanitarian prison reformer, publicly advocated the practice of charity: nevertheless, Howard at home was a tyrant. Burns in one or two of his poems gracefully praises the domestic virtues:

To make a happy fireside clime
For weans and wife,
That's the true pathos and sublime
Of human life.

But even his most ardent admirers would hardly describe Burns as a model of husbandly or fatherly behavior. The bare fact has to be faced that no merely human moral teacher ever wholly succeeds in bringing his character and conduct into complete conformity to his code. But Jesus does! Never once does he himself fall below the standard which he sets for others. He alone actualizes his ideal. Wherefore, preach Christ ethically, as Teacher and Example.

III

Preach him, finally, eschatologically, as destined Judge and Ruler of the world. No article in the so-called Apostles' Creed calls more clamorously for clarifying treatment in the pulpit of today than the stupendous statement: I believe that he will come. Paradoxically, one of the *first things* in a man's ministry ought to be the great doctrine of the *Last Things*. The age lacks a horizon. It does not know where it is going—though, like Huxley on the Dublin jaunting car, it does know that it is going somewhere at appalling speed!—and, almost frantic in its bewilderment, it desperately wants someone to fling back the curtains of the future and forecast the shape of things to come. Yet, queerly enough, in this matter the ministers of Christ, who alone have a right to speak, are often mute. Prophets of science are far readier with their confident prognostications than are prophets of the most high God. There are all sorts of fantastic speculations as to what is to be and as to how the world will end. Some say the earth will crack as a consequence of planetary collision, flying to pieces amid the whirling spheres. Some swear that it is swinging gradually nearer and nearer to the sun and that its human population is doomed to extinction in the solar fires. Some, on the contrary, maintain that the planet is drifting slowly farther and farther away from the source of its light and heat and that, within calculable time, it will be spinning vacantly through space, a vast rolling sepulcher, as cold and lifeless as its moon. This gloomy mood is reflected in the poetry of the period, as witness the following dreary line by T. S. Eliot:

> This is the way the world ends,
> This is the way the world ends,
> This is the way the world ends,
> Not with a bang but a whimper.[1]

In your preaching, nail that pitiful lie. Proclaim with fervor your profound conviction that, as Reinhold Niebuhr felicitously expresses it: "History is to have a worthy conclusion." The world is not going to end with a whimper. Nor is it going to end with a bang. It is going to end with a shout and with the voice of the archangel and with the trump of God. "There are many," cried John Wesley once, half-mocking, "who are anxiously asking: 'What will the end be? What will the end be?' Well," he went on, "what *shall* the end be? Why, glory to God in the Highest, on earth peace and goodwill amongst men!" "History is to have a worthy conclusion."

In this colossal climax of the historical drama Christ is to have a double role. He is to be Judge and he is to be King—Judge to right the iniquities of the past and King to insure the continuance of an equitable order in the future. That human actions, and even human thoughts, are to be brought at last to the bar of a great Tribunal is a fact to which most solemn testimony is borne in the New Testament. Yet it is not a fact which seems to influence men's conduct very much nowadays. Few appear consciously to relate their lives to any final standard of reference or to anticipate their appearance at the great Review. We are a long way now from Daniel Webster's

[1] From "The Hollow Men," *Collected Poems 1909-1935*. Used by permission of the publishers, Harcourt, Brace and Co.

haunting recollection of his personal accountability to God. But unless the Bible grievously misleads us, Jesus is to be our Judge. That sobering truth is reiterated again and again in scripture. It is set forth in parable and picture as well as in such plain, unequivocal statements as this of the apostle Paul in his address to the Athenians: "[God] hath appointed a day, in which he will judge the world in righteousness by that man whom he hath ordained." We are, therefore, in direct line with the teaching of the Bible when we repeat the clause of the ancient creed: I believe that he will come to be our Judge.

This is a note that needs sounding in the pulpit of today. Jesus is to be our Judge. Our lives matter morally. They are to have an ultimate ethical evaluation. At last they are to be subjected to the awful magistracy of the Most High. Bad behavior is not to be blamed upon heredity or "glands" or environment: it is to be charged upon the recalcitrant human will. We are responsible creatures, and that means not only that we are responsible *for* something but also that we are responsible *to* Someone, and that Someone is Jesus Christ. Strike that deep chord in your preaching and the hearts of your hearers will be filled with a fresh sense of the solemnity and dignity of human life.

Not only is Jesus to be Judge, however; he is also to be King. That is to be his second great role. And he is to be King not simply in the realm of eternal realities, as we have already noted, but likewise in the region of temporal affairs. As to the exciting certainty of Christ's ultimate universal sovereignty the Scriptures speak expressly. Several relevant proof-texts leap instantly to mind: "He must reign, till he hath put all enemies under his feet"; "The kingdoms of this world are become the kingdoms of our Lord, and of his Christ"; "Alleluia: for the Lord God omnipotent reigneth." With the establishment of this earthly Kingdom all that is best in the fine dreams of social philosophy—Plato's *Republic*, More's *Utopia*, Bacon's *New Atlantis*, and so on—will come splendidly true. At one stride they will pass out of the sphere of speculative idealism into that of practical politics. That is what makes this prospect so entrancing. For the trouble with all secular visions of the perfect state is that their fulfillment seems always to be postponed to some vague and indeterminate period in the future. They are like the skyline which recedes as you advance toward it; a circumstance from which, in cynical moods, we are apt to draw the deduction that they are unlikely to materialize at all.

In Glasgow I once conducted the funeral of a Communist agitator. He had been something of an orator and had gone from one part of the country to another passionately propagating his political creed. Every inch of him he had been Karl Marx's man, and, when he died, they had propped up the sagging jaw of his corpse with a huge copy of *Das Kapital.* But as I stood on that bleak January day by his open grave on the snow-covered hillside and saw the coffin slowly lowered into its narrow resting place, I was struck by the irony of it all, and beneath my breath I muttered: "Ah, poor fellow, of what use are all your utopian dreams to you now, your luring visions of an ideal social order; six feet of earth is all you've got forever!"

The kingdom of God, however, is different. Its nature is strangely paradoxical. It is to come, and yet it is here. It is future, and yet present. It is a hope, and yet a fact. Christian eschatology, as C. H. Dodd has taught us, is "realized eschatology." The kingdom has begun. "The kingdom of God," said Jesus, "is within you." "The kingdom of God," declared Paul, "is not meat and drink; but righteousness, and peace, and joy in the Holy Ghost." And once that radiant realm has been set up in your inmost being, once it is thoroughly established there, it becomes easy to believe—in truth, it becomes impossible not to believe!—that, despite all evidence to the contrary, that realm will yet be commensurate with the habitable globe, that

Nearer and nearer draws the time, the time that shall surely be,
When the earth shall be filled with the glory of God, as the waters cover the sea.

"This is the order in which the truth is mediated to faith," wrote Hugh Ross Mackintosh, "and in which case it is charged with power. We first recognize Christ as Lord within the range of individual personal life, and expand this initial assurance to universal and absolute dimensions." Because the kingdom has come, we are sure that it is coming.

But meantime what is to be our attitude? Are we to fold our arms or are we to roll up our sleeves? Opinions differ. "Fold your arms," say some. "Wait for the final hour. Tarry the leisure of the Lord"—a policy, if such it may be called, pilloried by John Major in his parody of the familiar hymn:

Sit down, O Men of God!
His Kingdom He will bring
Whenever it shall please His will:
You need not do a thing!

Is that to be our attitude? Or are we not rather to roll up our sleeves and address ourselves to the work? As J. Parton Millom has discerningly pointed out, there are really three ways in which men look for the establishment of the perfect state. There is the way of revolution; that is, by human action alone. There is the way of revelation; that is, by divine action alone. And, between these two, there is the way of co-operation, in which the divine and the human combine for the accomplishment of the social purpose. This last is the true method. It takes God and man to build the kingdom. On the one hand, we are to work for its coming—by evangelism, by legislation, by the exercise of our personal influence—as though everything depended upon us: on the other hand, we are to pray for its coming, as though everything depended upon God. And thus, by the joint endeavor of God and man, the kingdom will at last become a political reality and the government will rest upon his shoulder, whose right it is to reign. Preach Christ, then, eschatologically, as destined Judge and Ruler of the world.

IV

Now this conception of the nature and function of preaching seems to me to carry with it four immensely significant corollaries.

The first is obvious. It is *the personal content of Christian preaching*. There is a popular mode of presenting the gospel as though it were something almost purely factual—the proclamation of a series of historic happenings in virtual detachment from the Person to whom they happened. Thus it is common to speak of the Cross, of the Resurrection, and of Pentecost as though in themselves these things possessed some magical or mechanical potency quite apart from the One with whose career they were connected. Take up your New Testament, however, and you will find that there the chief stress is always laid not on the events themselves, momentous though they were, but rather on the Personality behind the events. For example, the primitive Christian preachers did not proclaim the crucifixion of Christ: they preached Christ and him crucified. They did not dilate on the resurrection of Jesus: they dwelt adoringly on Jesus and the Resurrection. They did not discuss the phenomena of Pentecost: they spoke of Christ by his Spirit indwelling the heart. Always the main emphasis was on the Personality. With this view of preaching in our minds, we see how inevitable that was; for if preaching be, in very truth, the communication *of* a Person *through* a person *to* a company of persons, it goes without saying that its theme can never be purely factual. It must be personal. In other words, it must be Christ. From first to last he must be the Burden of your ministry, and you are to be concerned with historical occurrences, however dramatic, spectacular, epoch-making, only because of their connection with him.

The second corollary is *the permanent relevance of Christian preaching*. That word "relevance" is the epidemic word in religious circles nowadays. It is on every lip. People talk about the "relevance" of the Bible, the "relevance" of the Church, the "relevance" of Christianity. James Denney and F. R. Barry started it, and now everybody has become infected. Prominent among the things thus put to the proof is preaching. Is preaching relevant? Is it relevant, for one thing, in view of the discoveries and inventions of modern science? Time was when the preacher was the dominant figure in the cultural life of the community. The "parson" was, as the appellation itself implies, the "person," or, as we should prefer to say, the "personality" in the social group to which he belonged, and his deliverances in the pulpit, whatever their intrinsic worth, were invested in the public mind, of that locality at least, with something like oracular authority. You have only to read the life of Richard Baxter of Kidderminster or that of Grimshaw of Haworth or that of Kidd of Aberdeen to realize for how much such men counted in the spheres in which they moved. Now it is far otherwise. The press, the radio, the cinema, and television discharge certain of the functions of the old-time preacher. And, of course, if that is all there is to it—if preaching is only a means of popularizing education or of broadcasting information, if, as I say, that is all there is to it—then we shall have to admit that its day is done and that its task is now better performed by other agencies. But *is* that all there is to it? Not by any means. Preaching, in the very nature of things, can never be superseded or surpassed. It has something to do which no press or radio or cinema or television apparatus in the world can possibly accomplish. It has to give Christ to the age, and it takes more than a machine to do that. No! Modern technological equipment may implement the work of preaching and widen its range; it can never supplant it or render it obsolete and irrelevant. For another thing, is preaching relevant in the light of the broader conceptions now current of the duties of a Christian minister? A generation or two back the minister was a preacher and little more. When Alexander Whyte began his ministry in Glasgow, the Kirk session told him bluntly that, if faced with the alternatives of answering a summons to visit the dying or preparing his Sunday sermon, and if he could do the one or the other but not both, he ought to prepare his Sunday sermon. Such was the place then popularly assigned in the churches to the ministry of the Word. How different now! The minister is still a preacher, to be sure, but in the majority of cases he is called upon to be a score of things besides—organizer, secretary, psychiatrist, youth-club leader, and what will you? Among so many competing claims how is he to allocate the hours of each day and to what is he to devote his finest energies? He cannot give his best to all. Some sort of discrimination and selection there must be. What is to have priority, the lion's share of his talents and his time? Plainly the answer will be determined by what he considers most deserving and likely to be most rewarding. It will be surprising if he focuses his main force on preaching unless he sincerely believes that preaching is the biggest job he has on hand. But is it? That depends on your conception of preaching. Nor can it be denied that there are not wanting those today who are only too ready to disparage it. Differentiating between the minister who is a "work-man" and the minister who, they say, is a mere "word man," they draw invidious distinctions between them, much to the disadvantage of the latter. A "word man"! "What is a word?" asks Stalker, and he answers: "It is only a puff of air, a vibration trembling in the atmosphere for a moment and then disappearing." Well, if we accept that definition, and if preaching be no more than words, words, words, then manifestly it is possible to achieve something uncommonly like it by merely manipulating a pair of bellows! But if preaching be in truth the transmission of *the* Word—ah, then, no minister need ever be ashamed to be spoken of as a "Word man," for that is his specific calling, his distinctive privilege. For yet another thing, is preaching relevant in view of veering modes of modern Protestant public worship? The replacement of the pulpit by the altar in the central position in so many of our churches is more than a mere architectural fashion, a passing fad in the furnishing and decoration of ecclesiastical edifices: it is symptomatic of a trend in current theological thought. What is happening is this, that preaching, that "royal ordinance," as Edward Irving called it, is being set on one side in favor of the drapery and carpentry of a theatrical religious externalism. Confessedly there was a tendency in certain of the Reformed churches to promote preaching to a position in the services of the sanctuary to the detriment of other parts of public worship, these last being reduced to the level of—dreadful word!—"preliminaries." In some quarters folk tended to fall down before the preacher as Cornelius fell before Peter. That is indefensible. Yet is it not far more likely that God will come to meet the people through a living personality than through a dead altar? White candles winking on silver stands, gorgeous tapestries, richly embroidered altar cloths, the delicate tracery of a screen or the exquisite carving of a reredos—these are, after all, mere things: beautiful things, doubtless, appealing strongly to the artistic sense and satisfying for the time the aesthetic demands of our nature, yet still only things. Not before them are we most powerfully constrained to bow, but before the Word, when that Word is conceived of as a Person and conveyed by the Spirit through the instrumentality of a consecrated preacher. Preaching is, therefore, still centrally relevant despite the changes in the modes of public worship.

Pass now to the third corollary. It is *the indispensable prerequisite to Christian preaching*. On this topic I have touched before and I shall have occasion to refer to it again; but it may not be out of place to make a few comments here also on a matter of such cardinal importance. "The indispensable prerequisite to Christian preaching." What is that? Is it what we call "personality"? No. Is it the orator's gift? No. Is it the mystic's sensitivity? No. Is it college training? No. Is it the possession of theological knowledge? No. What, then, is it? Open your New Testament. Turn to that dazzling passage where, having risen triumphant from the tomb, the Master appears to his disciples and talks to them about what they are to do for him in the future. A large part of their service is to consist of preaching. Yet, strangely enough, they are not to begin straight away. They are to wait for a while. "Tarry ye!" he commands. Now why? What is the reason for this prohibition? Several of them at any rate are men of outstanding personality, but they are not to preach. Some are most movingly eloquent, but they are not to preach. One of them for certain is dowered with mystic vision. Yet they are not to preach. All have spent perhaps three years in Jesus' college, the finest divinity seminary ever known. Yet they are not to preach. John has stood beneath the cross, and he and Peter have stared into the empty sepulcher. Yet they are not to preach. Why? There can only be one answer. They have not yet been filled with the Holy Spirit. The Jesus of history has not yet been for them Pentecostally transformed into the Christ of experience, and they cannot convey him whom they have not received.

Let us look more narrowly at the scene. Behind barred doors in an Upper Room at Jerusalem a band of men are herded together, like frightened sheep in a pen. They have heard strange rumors that Jesus has risen from the dead, but they cannot bring themselves to believe them. And then, suddenly, blazing into visibility in their very midst, comes the living Christ. At first dazed and terrified by the spectacle, his followers at length grow calm as he breathes his peace upon them. Gradually the reality of what they are witnessing begins to dawn upon their minds, and this unexpected return of their Master becomes doubly welcome to these disappointed men. It is welcome most of all because it is a reunion with One whom they warmly love and whom they never thought to see again. But it is welcome also for a further reason, because in it they beheld the pledge of the fulfillment of those romantic dreams of theirs as to what Christ was going to be and to do in the world. "Lord," they inquire, "wilt thou at this time restore again the kingdom to Israel?" This now seems a practical proposition, after all. For if, while still subject to the limitations of his incarnate life, Jesus wrought such marvels, what may he not do now that the Resurrection has released him from those hampering handicaps and invested him with imperial power? "Lord," they keep asking, eagerly, excitedly, "wilt thou? Wilt thou?" Jesus looks them inspiringly in the eyes and says something that sends a tremor through their very souls. "*Ye* shall," he says. "All that I was wont to do before I went to the cross, all that I am able to do now that I am risen from the dead, you shall accomplish when you receive the dynamic from on High." This is what as preachers they are to tarry for. This is to be their qualifying endowment, their enabling gift. The real power in preaching stems from one thing and from one thing only—that mighty rushing wind that struck the first disciples in the Upper Room. That is the indispensable prerequisite to Christian preaching.

The fourth and final corollary is *the appropriate response to Christian preaching*. Here you have another inevitable deduction from our premises, a necessary inference from the facts. As preachers your primary task will not be to inform the minds nor to kindle the imaginations nor even to touch the hearts of your hearers—though you will, of course, do all that in the exercise of your ministry—your primary task will be to get them to open their beings to the living Jesus. Were Christianity just a set of dogmatic propositions, a collection of theological theories, it might suffice to win an intellectual assent to it and to leave it at that. But no. You dare not do so. For, if the content of your preaching be personal, there can be but one adequate and appropriate response to it from those to whom it is addressed—the response of acceptance of the Christ it seeks to convey. When you have persuaded your hearers to do that, your work is done, your ordeal over: your Burden has become their blessing.

Chapter Two

THE MAN

AMONG THE PROBATIONERS admitted to the old Congregational College at Bradford, Yorkshire, in September, 1882, was a young student whose preaching was destined to take the world by storm. He was John Henry Jowett. Some time later it fell to his lot to preach in sermon class one day before his fellow students and under the presidency of the distinguished principal, Dr. Andrew Fairbairn. When he had ended, the students were invited to criticize his effort. They did; handling it pretty roughly, after the ruthless custom of their kind, pointing out with naked candor the faults in its construction and the defects in its delivery. Fairbairn listened patiently until they had had their say. Then, summing up, he remarked: "Gentlemen, I will tell you what I have observed this morning. Behind that sermon there is a man!"

Few things matter more in preaching than the man at the back of it. About that the great preachers themselves leave us in no manner of doubt. So impressed indeed are some of them with its crucial significance that they actually tend to make too much of it. "Manhood," says Henry Ward Beecher, "is the best sermon." "The most important thing about a sermon," declares Joseph Parker, "is the man behind it." Now that is not so. The most important thing about a sermon is not the man behind it but the Christ within it, not the person preaching but the Person preached. P. T. Forsyth's reminder is, therefore, entirely to the point: "No man has any right in the pulpit in virtue of his personality or manhood in itself, but only in the sacramental value of his personality for his message. . . . The Church does not live by its preachers but by its Word." Yet Parker's exaggeration is almost excusable, for the personality of the preacher is indubitably a factor of prime moment in the presentation of the message.

This demand that the minister of Christ, whatever else he may or may not be, shall at all events be a man is something which may be said, in one view of it at least, to be distinctively modern. What James Stalker stated to be true of his own generation is even more strikingly apposite today:

> Ours is a democratic age; and this means that the minds of men are less and less influenced by merely hereditary and official distinctions and bestow their esteem only where they recognize personal merit. Formerly it was enough if a man was a king or noble. Now people ask: "Is he a kingly man? Is he himself noble?"

A clergyman, writing to the clergy, has said:

> Not long ago, a minister was certain of honour because he belonged to the clerical order and wore the clerical garb; as the saying goes, people respected the cloth. But this is rapidly passing away. Respect for ministers who are worthy of the name is not, indeed, passing away: it was never greater. But people no longer respect the cloth unless there is a man inside it. If a minister is to be loved and revered, he must be able to dispense with all artificial cubits added to his stature and, coming down among men and standing side by side with them, allow his manhood to be compared with theirs.

In other words, behind the message there must be a man.

It is a fact whose meaning must not be missed that the men who have most moved the masses to Christ in modern times have been the great humans, not the great divines. George Whitefield, Rowland Hill, Charles Haddon Spurgeon, Dwight L. Moody, John McNeill—all influenced the crowds by their humanity as no theological pedant ever did by his divinity. The preacher must perforce be a man.

But what sort of man? If preaching be, in sober fact, the communication *of* a Person *through* a person *to* a company of persons, then it follows naturally and by an inescapable logic that the kind of personality requisite in the preacher is the type through which Christ can be transmitted to mankind. Nothing less will suffice. Let me not hesitate to say it. A man may be veritably glittering with oratorical gifts, he may seem above most "to have what it takes" to be a minister, but if his character be such that he is not fitted to discharge homiletically the function fulfilled physically by Mary long ago, he can never be a true preacher.

What manner of man, then, is this whom Christ can use for the mediation of his personality in the act of preaching? Let us anatomize him and note some of his outstanding qualities and qualifications. We will study him from three standpoints: first, *in his natural attributes;* next, *in his spiritual prerequisites;* and then, *in his official capacity.*

I

We begin with *his natural attributes.* Although for most men some measure of expert instructon in the art and craft of preaching is absolutely essential—and the more they can have of it the better—yet all do not start, if one may put it so, "from scratch." Some are more adapted to the work than others and so commence with an immense advantage.

What are these natural attributes?

A commanding presence. Let me lead off with that. It would be idle to deny that the personal appearance of a minister is undoubtedly of considerable consequence in preaching. Chastely chiseled features, a leonine head, a courtly carriage—all these unquestionably predispose an audience in a preacher's favor. Does anyone seriously doubt that the classic beauty of the face of Alexander Whyte, the piercing eagle eye and sharp-cut profile of Alexander Maclaren, the angelic transparency of the countenance of the youthful R. J. Campbell had much to do with the pulpit success of their possessors? Beyond all cavil, physical factors do play a big part in preaching.

Yet it would be easy to overestimate their importance. James Black has, in truth, told us—and on this topic his word ought to carry as much weight as that of any!—that although at the beginning of a sermon an attractive appearance may establish a preacher in the good graces of the people, unless he has something vital and gripping to say that very thing may easily in the end tip the scale the other way. A handsome presence awakens fond hopes in the hearts of the hearers, and woe to the preacher if he fail to fulfill them!

Be that as it may, it is heartening to reflect that some of the foremost pulpit figures of the past seem to have contrived to rub along tolerably well without it. Is it merely coincidence, one wonders, that so many of them were marred by optical obliquity or other such abnormality? John Newton, George Whitefield, Edward Irving—each had a glaring squint. Christmas Evans fared even worse. At the height of his popularity he had but one eye. What a sight he must have been, standing up before the people, his one eye blazing, as with a rag dipped in laudanum he dabbed the empty socket of the other to ease the terrific pain! Yet, despite their disfigurement, these men moved the multitudes to Christ.

Chrysostom was no Apollo if an ancient pen-portrait does not libel him: "He was low of stature, his head was big, but entirely bald, his forehead large and full of wrinkles: still more singular, his eyes were not prominent but deep-set, sunk inwards." Nor is the picture which Henry Cockburn limns of Thomas Chalmers in any wise flattering to its subject: "He is awkward, and has a low husky voice, a guttural articulation, a whitish eye, and a large dingy countenance." On a level with these is Tulloch's portrayal of Charles Haddon Spurgeon. Describing a visit he had paid to the Surrey Gardens Music Hall to hear the great preacher, Tulloch wrote: "He improves a little in looks as he warms in preaching. At first he certainly is not interesting in face or figure—very fat and podgy. But there is no doubt of the fellow, look as he may." Such were some of the preachers who, in earlier times, won the crowds for Christ. On whatever other faculties likely to lead to popularity in preaching they might perhaps have boasted, it is plain that they owed little to bodily charm.

It must, of course, be recognized that physical attractiveness arises from one or other (or both) of two things. Either it is an accident of nature or it is a moral product. In the former sense a preacher may not be able to pride himself on the possession of much of it—all the better if he can!—but the latter he ought by the grace of God to do his diligence to acquire. After all, it is more important for a preacher to look good than to have what are commonly called "good looks." On learning that Brownlow North, till then a notorious libertine, was converted and had turned preacher, someone brutally remarked: "He will need a new face!" Thank God, he got it! For Christ has a wonderful way of transfiguring those who give their lives to the task of transmitting him. Erskine of Linlathen, a keen but kindly critic, was confirmed in his antipathy to Roman Catholicism because, as he reported, during a prolonged and extensive tour of Italy he had failed to find among its many devotees, clerical and lay, with whom in his travels he had come in contact, a single markedly spiritual countenance; whereas, on the other hand, even so neutral an observer as Charles Lamb was forced to pay tribute to the moral worth of Quakerism, since in its assemblies he had, as he vividly expressed it, "seen faces upon which the Dove sat visibly brooding." This last is the kind of countenance a preacher ought to covet, and it is not so much the gift of nature as a growth of grace. A glowing spirit will glorify the plainest countenance, and people will forget our features when we bare our hearts.

Another natural attribute which has stood preachers in good stead in past generations is *stately stature*. Many of the leading pulpit figures of bygone days were indebted for some at least of their professional impressiveness to their magnificent physiques.

Thomas Guthrie was six feet two; Edward Irving, six feet four; Charles G. Finney, nigh on seven feet. But, for the consolation of those who do not belong to the house and lineage of Goliath, it is only fair to say that there have been other preachers, as great as these if not greater, who fell far below the average height. Paul was a dwarf—measuring, it is said, a bare four feet six. Calvin was less than five feet. John Wesley was diminutive. Yet I defy you to find in history three mightier men. Isaac Watts belonged to the same breed, and in the following lines voiced a vigorous protest against the popular practice of judging a man by his mere size:

> I must be measured by my soul:
> The mind's the standard of the man.

In the pulpit, at least, Watts need have had no fear; for *there* the Christ is the standard of the man, and, if a preacher only mediate to the people the living Jesus, they will readily forgive him his physical defects.

A *good carrying voice.* That is a third desideratum. Its importance is obvious. The odd fact has, of course, to be faced that some of the princeliest preachers of the past have achieved distinction as pulpit orators although afflicted in early life with an embarrassing stammer. Chrysostom labored under this incapacity for years. Henry Ward Beecher, as a lad, had an impediment in his speech. Charles Kingsley had a horrible stutter. Yet these men mastered their crippling handicap and came in time to be accomplished speakers. It would seem, nevertheless, that there are certain clearly marked limits to what is compassable along this line. As W. E. Sangster pungently comments: "To put it at its crudest, one knows that God made a mighty evangelist of a man with an awful squint (in George Whitefield), but one knows of no instance of God making a public evangelist of a man with a cleft palate or an *uncured* impediment of speech."

A good carrying voice is patently indispensable to effective preaching. "Courage, brother, do not *mumble*" may be capital advice to the bashful young preacher, but how if he lack the requisite vocal apparatus?

You will notice I am taking it for granted that in preaching you *will* employ your voice. May I remind you of Spurgeon's Dickensian dictum: "Avoid the use of the nose as an organ of speech, for the best authorities are agreed that it is intended to smell with"? Spurgeon himself certainly did not preach nasally. "His voice," said one who had heard him, "is of rare felicity, as clear as a bell—not a syllable lost." Of Joseph Parker it is told that his tones in the pulpit were like those of a mighty organ, thundering and reverberating through the City Temple and filling every corner of the vast building with its matchless music. And so very flexible and delicate an instrument was the voice of Whitefield that Garrick, the actor, declared that he would gladly give all he possessed to be able to say "Oh," as Whitefield said it.

Need I pause to point out that I am not pleading for mere vocal volume or contending that leather lungs are the main thing in the ministry? Mere noise is nothing. Any schoolboy can make that. Stentorian tones are not essential in the preacher, but an adequate voice of some sort he plainly must possess if he is to make himself heard in the pulpit at all; and it goes without saying that the finer his native faculty in this direction the better. Still, if nature has not gifted us with the power of mellifluous speech, it is well-nigh incredible what training can accomplish—although, of course, it has its limits! Elocution is indeed a cunning art, and one hesitates to say offhand what it can or cannot do; but one may perhaps be pardoned for concluding that not even its most proficient practitioner is likely, for all his cleverness, to be capable of transforming a croaking crow into a trilling lark! When you come to think of it, the very term "voice production" is a misnomer. It cannot really *produce* the voice; it can only *educe* it. The indigenous faculty must be there from the start.

A fourth desirable natural attribute in the preacher is *competent mental equipment*. No candid and impartial observer of the contemporary religious scene would be likely to contend that the pulpit today is devoid of intellectual power. On the contrary, it is probably true to say that the general level of mental capacity in the ministry was never higher. There may be fewer intellectual giants in the pulpits, but the common run of ministers are mentally much taller than, say, their Victorian counterparts. Even a casual glance through the relevant literature of the two periods serves to put it beyond all reasonable cavil that the sermons of the present generation far surpass in intellectual quality those of a hundred years ago.

Now, however, it has to be said, the pendulum has swung too far in the opposite direction. The prevailing tendency is to make too much of mere mind. A large part of the trouble with the modern Church, as I see it, is that the Areopagites have got into the pulpits—men not really gripped by the great saving verities of the gospel but simply bent on saying some new thing. One can well imagine that if certain present-day preachers had gone to Athens long ago, as did Paul, they would not have got up on the rostrum and begun to expound their own distinctive message: more probably, they would have sat down at the feet of the pagan philosophers and meekly begged to be informed as to their latest speculations. Not so the great apostle. In the intellectual capital of the world he did not go cap in hand to the proud protagonists of a secular culture: he carried his flaming message to the top of Mars Hill and flung it like a blazing torch in the midst of the academicians, for them to make of it what they might. The glorious irony of it is, of course, that, despise him as they might and did, his was the mightiest intellect of them all. Yet it was not a consciousness of intellectual superiority which made him thus courageous in confronting the sages of ancient Greece: it was an invincible conviction of the grandeur of his theme and of the loyalty of his companioning Lord. What a tragedy when the preacher licks the boots of the philosopher and gets kicked by them for his pains! Such, it must be owned, is the fault and fate of many nowadays. Cleverness, in some quarters, has come to be more highly rated than holiness, and intellectual brilliance than humble devotion to Christ.

In view of this it may be permissible to point out what is indeed writ large across the face of Christian history, that some of the ablest preachers of the past were men of very slender mental apparatus and of almost no specialized training.

Take D. L. Moody, for example. He was almost utterly unschooled. So illiterate was he as to be capable of using in public address the shocking phrase "the Spirit done it," and all his manuscripts had to be carefully edited before publication to eliminate barbaric breaches of grammar. Or take William Booth. His official biographer, St. John Ervine, writes:

> In 1885 Booth took his Bible and an umbrella, and stood on Mile End Waste, a broad patch of derelict land which lay at the side of Mile End Road, Whitechapel, where he preached, sometimes in front of The Vine public-house, and sometimes in front of The Blind Beggar. He could not foresee what he was doing when he banged his Bible and waved his umbrella to attract attention, and uttered his simple faith in a harsh, uneducated voice which scattered aitches as the wind scatters dust, but then he began one of the greatest religious organizations in the world.

Or take Charles Haddon Spurgeon. He was not, at least in early life, what would commonly be called a cultured man. Like Shakespeare and many another, he had "small Latin and less Greek"—though when preaching in later years, he dearly loved a Latin tag! But he had no specialized theological training, save what he may have picked up from his ministerial grandfather. Yet name me three other men who have exercised a more world-shaking ministry in modern times! Intellect, therefore, is not the principal thing.

Intellectuality is desirable in a preacher only when it is consecrated intellectuality—the intellectuality of a Paul, a Calvin, a

Chalmers. Otherwise, it can be a positive nuisance. Wycliffe stated the fact with blunt frankness: "An unlettered man with God's grace can do more for the Church than many graduates." Of John the Baptist an old Puritan dryly remarked that "he had preached to far more people with his head off than ever he did with it on." One has known other preachers whose range of pulpit influence might have been similarly extended by *metaphorical* decapitation.

Needless to say, this is not to decry intellect as such. Dedicated to the service of Christ, it is an offering "holy, acceptable unto God." On such conditions we cannot have too much of it. Is there anywhere a sight more deeply moving than that of a man laden with gifts, laying them all humbly and adoringly at the Redeemer's feet? And that, after all, is where they were meant to be. In the words of a wise old Welsh divine: "Hebrew, Greek and Latin are all very well in their place; but their place is not where Pilate put them, over Jesus' head, but rather at His feet."

A fifth natural faculty in the preacher should be *a capacity for hard work.* One of the minor miseries of the ministry is to be working yourself to death while popularly supposed to be having the time of your life. Let me say outright that no man who is not prepared to work himself to death has any right in the ministry at all. Where is there a more despicable creature than he who spares himself in the cause of Christ? And how can one who is habitually taking things easy convincingly preach the gospel of the Cross? The thing just cannot be done. "My Father worketh hitherto, and I work," said Jesus. You cannot be Christlike unless you are a worker. Broadly speaking, I suspect that in this respect men fall into one or other of two categories: either they work that they may rest or they rest that they may work. There may not seem, for all practical purposes, to be much to choose between them, but in the domain of motive they are miles apart. To the one, toil is a necessary evil; to the other, it is a sheer delight. The preacher must belong to the second class. He must take pride and find pleasure in his task. For true preaching is the most exacting labor in the world, and a man can make nothing of it unless he puts everything into it. In their preparations for the pulpit the old Puritans knew well how to roll up their mental sleeves. There was nothing in the least slipshod or slatternly about their homiletical workmanship. Some of them studied for as many as fourteen hours a day and one of them, at any rate, was so busy with his books that he could not so much as find time to get wed! John Wesley did not make matters quite so difficult for his preachers, but he would not suffer any man to minister in his societies unless he undertook to devote a minimum of five hours in every twenty-four to diligent delving in the Word of God. "Kill yourselves with work," was Spurgeon's sage advice to his students, "and then pray yourselves alive again."

Giving birth to the Word cost Mary something. Dare any preacher deserving of the name expect to discharge his holy duty cheaply? Was not Joseph Parker right when he averred that true preaching is "the sweating of blood"? Of Howell Harris, the gallant Welsh evangelist, it is told that, though only twenty-four, albeit a man of Herculean physique, he had so worn himself out with preaching that "when he went before a congregation he could hardly stand on account of weakness." After pouring out his soul in the pulpit, passionately pleading with sinners, George Whitefield would often be found prostrate in extreme exhaustion on the vestry floor. Yet here, as elsewhere, is not the Master himself our supreme model and exemplar? What days of toil were his! What nights of laboring prayer! Three years in the ministry made an old man of him. "Thou art not yet fifty years old," they said, making a rough guess at his age. Fifty! He was only thirty! I will make no secret of it.

True preaching takes the life out of you. It is my sober judgment that every real sermon that a man preaches appreciably shortens his days. But is not that, after all, as it should be? For who that has a heart for Christ at all can help spending himself and being spent in so glorious a cause?

To say that is not to deny his right to regular relaxation. There is a wise saying that we can sometimes do more by doing less. "The time is not wasted that a mower spends in whetting his scythe." For invigorating recreation there is a legitimate and even a necessary place. We have the authority of James Stalker for the statement that to rest on Monday is for the preacher a religious duty since he cannot rest on Sunday—a sentiment which Jonathan Swift endorses, describing Monday as "the parsons' holiday."

There is a good deal to be said in this connection for what has been called "the sandwich idea"—making Sunday a day of toil between two days of comparative rest, Saturday being spent in spiritual preparation and Monday in physical relaxation. Still, if you are a true preacher, you will probably find it hard even on Mondays not to be about your business. Of Phillips Brooks it is said that then he had his friends around him:

> It was his day of rest, but through all the conversation he never lost sight of the sermon-idea which had inspired him. On the mornings of Monday and Tuesday he was bringing together in his notebook, or on scraps of paper, the thoughts which were cognate to his leading thought, or necessary for its illustration and expansion, collecting the material for his sermon.

To the same purpose was Joseph Parker's keen rejoinder to the lady who asked: "What is your hobby, Dr. Parker?"

"Preaching!"

"But I mean in addition to preaching."

"Preaching, nothing but preaching; everything with me ministers to preaching!"

Personally I consider it a capital plan to spend Monday attending to practical chores—answering letters (Napoleon, to be sure, maintained that if you left them unanswered for a fortnight, you generally found that they had answered themselves, but it is unsafe for the minister to proceed upon this principle!), dealing with business affairs, undertaking rather more than the usual pastoral visitation, and so on. Here you have a fine way of easing a mind habituated to stiff intellectual toil. Yet doubtless you will often find it more rewarding still to let the brain lie absolutely fallow for a while each week, cultivating what Wordsworth called a "wise passiveness," and doing simply nothing at all. Learn that there are times when it is not lax to relax. For then you are merely "resting" your mental soil for the sowing of fresh seed.

A further qualifying attribute in the preacher is *the human touch.* You cannot get far in the ministry without that—the tact that makes for contact. One thinks in this connection of Edward Irving's calling on the Glasgow cobbler and conversing with him so knowledgeably about his craft—Irving's own father having been a tanner—that later the shoemaker was fain to declare: "He's a real sensible man, yon: he kens aboot leather." One thinks, too, of Norman Macleod smothered in the smoke of the smithy as he chatted in friendly fashion with the farrier and of how the latter afterward confessed: "He never came into my shop without talking to me as if he had been a blacksmith all his life." One thinks, most of all, of Jesus beckoning his first disciples to follow him as they stood mending their nets, in the knee-deep surf, and of how, in summoning them to the new life, he pictured it in terms likeliest to take a fisherman's fancy—as a matter of *fishing* for men! That is a true witness which is borne to him in *The Letters of James Smetham:*

> Christ takes your view of things and mentions no other. He takes the old woman's view of things, and shows a great interest in wash-powder; Sir Isaac Newton's view of things, and wings among the stars with him; the artist's view of things, and feeds among the lilies; the lawyer's, and shares the justice of things. But He never plays the lawyer, or the philosopher, or the artist to the old woman. He is above that littleness.

In other words—if indeed it be not verging on the indecorous to say so—Jesus was an adept at establishing social contacts, a master of the human touch. He possessed in perfection the faculty some have for getting at one stroke straight to people's hearts. Happy is the minister who has it.

A final natural attribute of the preacher is *imaginative power*. I do not say this is indispensable, for many eminently useful preachers appear to have been totally devoid of it; but I do say that, if exercised with delicacy and restraint, it can be an extraordinary advantage to the servant of the Word. Most of the popular pulpit figures have excelled in it. Here, for instance, is old Gilfillan, discoursing in his pulpit in Dundee on that breathless episode in the life of Paul when he was let down over the wall of Lystra in a basket; the preacher, meanwhile, utterly lost in his theme, leaning over the rail, paying out an imaginary rope very gingerly, and gazing downward with apparent apprehension as if to guard the basket from grazings and bumps against the wall, and shouting all the while: "Take care, there! Take care! The future of European civilization is dangling on that rope!" Or here is Williams of Wern, a worthy of the old Welsh pulpit, preaching from the window of a chapel in Merthyr Tidvil to a huge throng that, unable to gain admittance to the building, has gathered to hear him in the churchyard without. His theme is a thrilling one—the resurrection of the dead—and as he warms to his subject, handling it with massive power, he so grips the imagination of the crowd that when, with vivid realism, he tells of the pealing trumpet, the bursting tombs, the rising bodies, the people huddle together in terror, staring awe-struck at the sod beneath their feet, as if expecting the graves to open there and then and disgorge the sheeted dead! Or here is Alexander Whyte, preaching in the pulpit of the then Free St. George's, Edinburgh. His topic is the final overthrow of evil, its complete and irretrievable expulsion from the universe; of this he finds a striking forecast in the story of the casting forth of the wicked angels from the presence of God. With Miltonic grandeur he pictures the epic struggle between the opposing forces and shows how at last the evil hosts were utterly routed and hurled in confusion over the battlements of heaven. Graphically the great preacher depicts their headlong descent to the red regions below. Then, swiftly discarding the elevated tone and dropping his voice to a whisper, he adds the terriffic aside: *"They are falling still!"* There you have the imaginative faculty in full play, a faculty which, more perhaps than any other, is likely to persuade a listless people to lend a preacher their ears.

Such, then, are seven natural attributes which give an enormous advantage to any man going into the ministry. Some of these attributes are indispensable; others are less important: but all are of priceless value.

II

Stepping, now, one pace further, let us proceed to study the preacher in *his spiritual prerequisites*. What sort of man must he be from this point of view?

First, I would say that he must be *a man conscious of a great call*. It was a mark of the courtesy of God in his dealings with Mary at the Incarnation that he did not leave her to infer her high motherhood from the functional changes in her body. That would have been unchivalrous; and the shock of the discovery, when at last it came, might well have been too much for her. But God did not act like that. To have done so would not have been consonant with his character, nor would it have been in keeping with his customary mode of treating his creatures. He broke the news to her beforehand, told her how it was to be with her, even sued for her consent. Before the Incarnation there was an Annunciation.

Always it is so likewise in the life of the true preacher. Depend upon it: if God means you for the ministry, he will tell you so himself. He will break the news to you personally. He will not suffer you simply to guess, to speculate, to conjecture: he will make you dead sure. You will know past all doubt that this and this alone is to be your personal destiny. You will hear the call.

Of John Paterson Struthers, the sainted and scholarly preacher of Greenock, a touching and strikingly impressive story is told which, strangely enough, has not found its way into either of the official biographies. It describes how, having completed a brilliant course at Glasgow University, he seemed curiously dilatory in entering upon his ministerial career. Clearly, with such abilities, he would have had small difficulty in securing a charge. Yet, contrary to Presbyterian usage. he did not at once apply to be taken on trial for license—a fact for which his fellow students found it hard to account. They could not make it out at all and at last one of them ventured to interrogate Struthers' mother on the point. "Why," he inquired, "is John so slow in launching out upon his vocation? Why doesn't he get on with his life-work?" For a moment she was dumb. Then, finger on lip, she whispered: "He's waiting for the Call!"

"Waiting for the Call." There can be no real beginning without that. J. H. Jowett declared,

> "I would affirm my conviction that in all genuine callings to the ministry, there is a sense of the divine initiative, a solemn communication of the divine will, a mysterious commission, which leaves a man no alternative, but which sets him in the road of this vocation bearing the ambassage of a servant and an instrument of the eternal God.

No real minister ever merely drifts into the work. Nor does he enter it simply because someone in a position of influence has, as we commonly say, "pulled the strings" for him. The only strings that are pulled in all genuine calls to the preacher's office are the heartstrings. And it is God who pulls them!

There are those, to be sure, who would discount out of hand all such claims to having received a divine call. "It is mere imagination," they would say, "pious imposture, the dramatization of personal desire, the rationalization of ambition, an affectation assumed by those who, strongly attracted to the ministerial life on other grounds, try to impart a religious color to their selfish designs by pretending to invest them with divine authority." How, in face of such searching criticism, is the preacher to maintain his conviction that God Almighty has called him to his holy function? Well, let him ask himself honestly what are his private reactions to the idea of being in the ministry. Does the prospect attract or repel him? Is he naturally drawn to it, or does he shy at it like a freightened horse? It is a striking and peculiarly significant fact that nearly all the great preachers of history have done just that. George F. Macleod says:

> The common experience of them all without exception is that not one of them wished to preach. Moses, who lived by faith and endured as seeing Him who is invisible, was prepared to do the whole bidding of God —except to speak. Isaiah, though he saw the whole glory of God, and the meaning of that glory for his day, yet begged to be excused from this one thing. Ezekiel pled that he might deliver his message in some other way. Chrysostom shrank from it for years. Augustine turned in every direction before he plunged. Luther might not have preached at all but for his vow of obedience, and that he was directly ordered so to do, for all his pleadings. John Knox was pressed into the ministry. Frederick Robertson begged to be excused. Not one of them tired of quoting St Paul, protesting their unfitness to the end.

To argue that, because a man happens to desire to preach, he is therefore not divinely intended to do so would be going too far. Yet the strange paradox would seem to be that one of the prime qualifications for the ministry is the deep personal feeling that one is not fit for it. That, surely, is as it should be. Because the moment we think we can do it, we are done for. Our humility is our security. From the beginning to the end of his professional career every true preacher is haunted by this sense of unworthiness and incapacity; and this, provided it does not paralyze him, is, as I say, a good thing, for it throws him back upon God and causes him ever to be humbly sensible of his utter dependence on the Most High. Make no mistake about it. There *is* such a thing as a personal call. Now, as in Jeremiah's time, it is true that in every genuine summons to the ministry "no man taketh this honour unto himself, but he that is called of God, as was Aaron."

Not always, of course, does the call come in precisely the same way or at the same stage in the private history of the person to whom it is addressed. Chalmers gave token of having heard it at three. Thus, early in his life he was discovered one day in his nursery at Anstruther declaiming with dramatic effect David's poignant lament on the death of Absalom. J. D. Jones claimed to have experienced the call at seven. More than half a century later he distinctly recalled preaching under some dim sense of it at that tender age in the playroom of their home in Cardiff to his little sister and a miscellaneous assortment of dolls. Alexander Maclaren declared that to his certain recollection there had never been a time when he had not felt that it was his mission to preach. To these men the great call came with the rising of the sun.

More commonly, however, it comes later. Indeed, not a few of Christ's foremost ministers of more recent times seem, like their primitive predecessors, to have been recruited from secular avocations when well into adult life. Jeremy Taylor was a hairdresser before he turned preacher. Thomas Guthrie was a bank clerk. Phillips Brooks started as a schoolteacher. John McNeill began as a railway employee. John Henry Jowett commenced as a solicitor's apprentice. In their cases the summons came tardily. As old Samuel Rutherford lamented in another connection, "the sun was high in the heaven before they took the gate by the end."

This variety in the moment and mode of the call's coming is amply illustrated in the Bible. Samuel was bidden as a boy, Isaiah as a youth, Moses as a mature man. Some heard the call amid the shimmering heat of the desert, some in cool groves where flowering fig trees grew. Some were surprised by the divine summons amid the silence of star-crowned shrines, some at tax collectors' tolls amid the bustle of busy seaports. Some, when the call came, were tending sheep on dreamy hills; some were thigh-deep in the foaming surf. The occasion and the hour differed in each instance: in all the call was the same.

So is it still. Let us review in rapid succession some of the ways in which the call comes to men in the modern world.

One is by *the compulsion of circumstances.* If God means to make a preacher of you, it is more than likely that he will bring the fact home to you by the pressure of events in your life, the thrust of things around you, the push and hustle of providential happenings. Quite frequently, at the time of their occurrences, these controlling circumstances appear trivial enough. Only in retrospect is their writ seen to have run so far in the realm of one's personal life.

Consider the classic case of F. W. Robertson. If we are to credit his own testimony, he became a preacher through the barking of a dog. The story has been often told. Actually, it seems, he had meant to be a soldier. There was a military tradition in the family and the love of battle was in his blood. The ring of trumpets, the thunder of guns, the march of armed men thrilled him to the marrow of his being. He applied for a commission in the army. Eagerly he awaited its arrival; but it did not come. Then, losing patience and concluding that the application had failed, he took his father's advice, matriculated at Oxford, and began to read for holy orders. Five days later the commission arrived. Robertson's feelings can better be imagined than described. He was bitterly disappointed. For a while his mind oscillated uncertainly between the alternative careers. At last, however, he resolved to decline the commission and to carry on with his theological studies. This decision he reached in rather an odd way. He afterwards explained,

> If I had not met a certain person, I should not have changed my profession; if I had not known a certain lady, I should not probably have

met this person; if that lady had not had a delicate daughter who was disturbed by the barking of my dog; if my dog had not barked that night, I should now have been in the dragoons or fertilizing the soil of India.

It looks like the merest chance: yet God used that seemingly casual contact to bring to birth in Robertson's mind the conviction that he was meant to be a minister.

A still more striking example is provided by the case of a very different type of personality—Peter Mackenzie, the old Methodist preacher. His biographer records that when but a youth Mackenzie had rashly undertaken to preach in a rural chapel. It was to be his first attempt. Naturally he was very nervous and as the day of the appointment drew nearer his trepidation increased alarmingly. At the time he was living in a two-roomed cottage in Durham, and, as the hour of the ordeal approached, he ran upstairs and flung himself on his knees upon the floor. Just then he heard three men enter the apartment below. They had come to accompany him to the chapel. Desperately he took up his Bible in the hope of obtaining guidance and did what he afterward declared he would not advise others in like circumstances to do, opened it, let the pages fall apart, and, shutting his eyes, put his finger on a text. Eager to see what it was, to his infinite astonishment he read: "While Peter [Mackenzie's name was Peter!] thought on the vision, the Spirit said unto him, Behold, three men seek thee. Arise therefore, and get thee down, and go with them, doubting nothing: for I have sent them." There, then, is one way in which the call may come to you—through the pressure of circumstances.

Here is another: it may come through *congregational constraint*. The fact that a company of Christ's people consider a man competent to preach and beg him to be their minister is not of itself an infallible guarantee that God means him for the ministry. The popular choice may be wrong.

You may recall that critically significant episode in the Book of Acts where, after the defection and suicide of Judas, the eleven remaining apostles had recourse to the ballot in an effort to settle upon his successor. The lot, you remember, fell upon Matthias. With suitable solemnity they ordained him. Laying hands upon him—*Peter's* hands among them!—they made him an apostle. But that is the last we hear of him. Matthias was a nonentity. Man-made apostles always are. And meanwhile God was urgently at work in the soul of a young man whose name was Saul. Emphatically, therefore, election to the ministry by popular suffrage is no infallible proof of having received a divine call.

Yet it is a plain matter of history that the call, confirmed in other ways, has come home compellingly to the hearts of some men through congregational constraint. There was a memorable May Sunday in a church at St. Andrews when John Rough, formerly chaplain to the earl of Arran, preached on the right of a Christian congregation to elect its own minister. John Knox was there. Breaking off dramatically in the midst of his sermon, Rough appealed directly to Knox in the hearing of the people. "Take upon you the public office and charge of preaching," he adjured him, "even as you look to avoid God's heavy displeasure." The congregation ratified the call. Rough was, indeed, only voicing their collective vote. "Whereat," says the chronicler quaintly, "the said John, abashed, burst forth in most abundant tears and withdrew himself to his chamber." The call may come through congregational constraint.

Furthermore, it may come through *prophetic intimation.* Reading the lives of famous preachers, one is often struck by the fact that so many of them, when young, had their future pulpit eminence foretold by saintly souls of their acquaintance who seem, consciously or unconsciously, to have donned the seer's mantle in so doing. Allowing for the apocryphal element in such tales and recollecting that, when a man has become great in any branch of human activity, those who had the honor of knowing him in boyhood frequently display an understandable tendency to romanticize those early years and to read back into them much that was not really there—allowing, I say, for such things, it does nevertheless seem as though in many instances the stories are substantially true.

Occasionally, to be sure, such forecasts were little more than pretty safe guesses. There was, for example, the case of Joseph Parker. Walking once as a lad with his father along a country lane near his native Hexham in Northumberland, he strolled on leisurely enough for a while; then suddenly he stopped and, standing by a gate, pointed to the glorious pomp of the clouds far above in the summer sky and, in a loud and sonorous tone, declaimed: "What are these arrayed in white, bright as the noonday sun?" Hearing which, his father there and then prophesied for him a dazzling career as a preacher—a prognostication not perhaps wholly attributable to paternal prejudice and wishful thinking.

More convincing, however, are forecasts of this kind uttered at a time when, so far as the records show, no such promise was as yet manifested by those about whom they were made. D. L. Moody, the evangelist, was preaching once to a vast crowd from an open carriage in a country district of England. Among the listeners was a wild gipsy lad who, having climbed on to a wheel of the vehicle, was hanging with breathless interest on every word the preacher spoke. There was nothing exceptional about the boy, but Moody was moved to prophesy concerning him. Laying his hand on the lad's bushy curls, he predicted that he would grow up to be a great evangelist. So it transpired. For the boy was Gipsy Smith.

Does not such a remarkable forecast bring to brilliant focus in our minds that lovely picture in the gospel of the aged Simeon proclaiming the destiny of the infant Christ, as he reverently holds him in his arms, and does it not also recall that historically decisive passage in the Acts which relates the circumstances surrounding the call of Saul of Tarsus?

Now there were in the church that was at Antioch certain prophets and teachers; as Barnabas, and Simeon that was called Niger, and Lucius of Cyrene, and Manaen, which had been brought up with Herod the tetrarch, and Saul. As they ministered to the Lord and fasted, the Holy Ghost said, Separate me Barnabas and Saul for the work whereunto I have called them.

The call may come through prophetic intimation.

These, then, are three modes in which the irresistible conviction that you are divinely meant for the ministry may be brought to bear upon you. Their witness, singly or cumulatively borne, can be commandingly convincing. Beyond all this, however, and complementary to it, are two vitally important things: *an inner impression* and *an outward confirmation.*

First, *an inner impression.* It is worth noting that when the time came for the Incarnation it was not to the Hebrew nation as a whole that the fact that Mary was to be the mother of the Messiah was conveyed, nor was it to some esoteric coterie of ecclesiastics learned in the rabbinical lore. The angel of the Annunciation did not proclaim his thrilling tidings to the world at large, nor did he secretly divulge them to the theological faculty of the university of Jerusalem: he went direct to Mary herself. As we have already had occasion to observe, she was told at first hand what was to happen to her, was personally and privately informed as to the divine purpose for her life. Not otherwise is it with the true preacher. Whatever objective evidence there may be that he is the recipient of a special call from God, clearer and, to him, more compelling than any is the subjective testimony of the Holy Spirit, the inward consciousness of the divine summons. Campbell Morgan maintains:

No man can go unless the Spirit call him. That is the high doctrine of the ministry—not even the Church, nor her theological halls. He must be called of the Spirit. Unless he hear that Call sounding in his soul, ringing like a trumpet night and day, giving him no rest until he is compelled to say: "Woe is me, if I preach not," then, in God's name, let him stay where he is, in his present calling. But, if he hear the Call, then let him remember that it is his business to go forward within the fellowship and under the guidance of the Church.

That is the inner impression.

But there is also *an outward confirmation*. If the Lord has indeed counted you faithful, putting you into the ministry, the fact will soon disclose itself. Your gift will make room for you; your apostleship will be sealed with many unmistakable signs; your profiting as a preacher will appear unto all. As someone has put it in a piquant epigram: "The best test of apostolical succession is apostolical success."

This point is brought out finely by the following familiar story. Lyman Beecher, as a youth, fell into conversation one day by the roadside with a farmer friend of his who was a convinced High Churchman. The farmer was mowing at the time and, as they chatted together, the talk turned to religion. "Mr. Beecher," said the farmer, "I should like to ask you a question. Our clergy says you are not ordained and have no right to preach. I should be glad to know what you think about it."

"Suppose," answered Beecher, "you had in the neighborhood a blacksmith who said he could prove that he belonged to a regular line of blacksmiths which had come down all the way from Peter, but he made scythes that did not cut; and suppose you had another blacksmith who said he did not see what descent from Peter had to do with making scythes, but he made implements that would cut: where would you go to get your scythes?"

"Why, certainly," replied the farmer, "to the man who made scythes that would cut."

"Well," said Beecher, "the ministry which cuts is the ministry which Christ has authorized to preach."

Ability in this matter is, in some sense, a proof of authority, for no man can truly minister unless the Lord be with him. In the case of every real preacher the outward results of his labors will always corroborate and confirm the inward impression that this and none other is his divinely intended task. The preacher will, then, in the first place, be a man conscious of a great call.

But more: he will be *a man expert through a great experience*. I do not mean that he will understand all mysteries and all knowledge, but that he will have passed through that profound spiritual transformation by means of which alone men are initiated into the deep things of God. Void of this a preacher, however valuable his views on other matters, is like a blind man talking about light or a deaf man about music. Paul states the fact with categorical finality: "The natural man receiveth not the things of the Spirit of God: for they are foolishness unto him: *neither can he know them.*" There you have it. The only true expositor is experience. Nothing can compound for failure to have undergone the great change. Better try lecturing on the politics of the planet Mars or minutely describing the habits of the pterodactyl than attempt to talk about the vast issues of Christian doctrine and experience without having known that radical revolution which is wrought in the human heart by the grace of God.

All powerful and persuasive preaching takes its rise in such a firsthand personal encounter with the truth. The pages of Christian biography provide not a few striking and impressive instances. I think, for example, of Henry Ward Beecher, lying in bed one night as a lad and meditating on the great matters of the soul, when, all at once, a light flashed in upon him and, leaping to the floor, his face aglow, he cried: "I have found it. I have found it! I have found the gospel!" I think, too, of Moody, gripped so mightily in his home one day by the thought of divine grace that he dashed out into the street and, accosting the first passer-by, seized him by the lapel of his coat and demanded: "Do you know what grace is?" I think, yet again, of the classic story of Dale, the great Congregational churchman of Birmingham, ruminating once on the fact of the resurrection of Jesus with a view to preparing an Easter sermon; and of how, as he churned the subject over in his mind, suddenly the irresistible conviction of its reality flamed in upon him, as it had never done before; and of how he got up and paced the floor of his study, exclaiming excitedly: "Christ is living! Christ is living! Living as really as I myself am!" In such peaks of passionate personal experience lay the springs from which later flowed in broad rivers the mighty ministries with which these men refreshed and fertilized the world. There is no substitute for the great change.

But what sort of a change is it? What precise difference does it make in a man's life? To that inquiry I would return three replies.

First, *it is a change from the sensual to the spiritual.* Modern life is very largely organized on the assumption that nothing matters very much but matter and that it is in the domain of the senses that the truest delights are to be found. The gratification of animal appetite, the satisfaction of carnal craving—these, we are told, constitute the best bliss earth has to offer. Now, as preachers, you are to deal a deathblow to that base slander upon life, and in the Bible, biography, the daily press, your own experience and observation of things, you have ample evidence lying ready to your hand to help you to refute it. But it is not enough in this regard to adopt a merely negative attitude, to inveigh against the vulgarity of sensuality. You must go further. You must personally exhibit and exemplify the high qualities which in your ministry you extol and inculcate. Nothing commends a preacher more to a discerning congregation than sparkling spirituality, the sort of personality which seems to be lit up from within. And it takes the great change to produce that. Nothing else can so move a man from the sensual to the spiritual.

Wrote A. W. Robinson:

Shortly before his death Lord Selbourne paid a visit to Wales and addressed a gathering of churchmen there. It was a time of much uncertainty, when many were anxiously wondering how the position of the Church in the Principality was to be upheld. The speaker said a great deal that was wise, but there was one counsel which, more than any others, fixed itself in the memories of his hearers. "Be spiritual," he urged. "Be spiritual. Be spiritual." That was the advice on which he insisted most earnestly, and never in all his life did the great lawyer give truer counsel than that.

"Be spiritual." Is it not Wilfred Grenfell who, in a fragment of recorded reminiscence, tells how after his conversion he could not endure to hear the gospel preached by a fat or self-indulgent-looking man? (Rather hard, that, on those who have trouble with their glands! but one sees what he means.) Instinctively he felt that he had a right to expect spirituality of the preacher. And, of course, he had! Preaching is, on one view of it, the vocalization of character. It is a life speaking. We do well, therefore, to remember for our hallowing that no man can simultaneously bear "the mark of the beast" and "the marks of the Lord Jesus." In common with every other practicing Christian the minister has with God's help to wage a desperate jungle warfare within. He has to fight lust and greed and sloth and a hundred other evil things on the secret battleground of his soul. But if he is not, through divine grace, winning the victory there, what message has he got for any other man? Unless all the flags are flying and all the trumpets blowing in his own heart, how can he ask others to follow him in the high crusade against sin? Do not, I beg you, deny your sermons the glow and the glory with which you might invest them were you to be inwardly conscious of the zest of living for the best. Spirituality is the great thing. Without it no man can preach with power: with it the preacher has diffused throughout his whole being the energies of omnipotence. His message rushes in among men, like a torrent from the hills, sweeping all resistlessly before it and bringing freshness and beauty wherever it goes. True pulpit power, however, is never merely a product of the pulpit. It breaks through in the pulpit, of course, flooding in like a mighty tide. But it never begins there. It begins far back in a life of disciplined spirituality. The great change is a change from the sensual to the spiritual.

Secondly, it is *a change from the selfish to the social.* How very seldom, in these pushful days, has one the good fortune to fall in with anyone whose life is truly animated by altruistic principles! Most people live for themselves. Some say so quite frankly. They tell you without a tremor that the only thing they are really bothered about is to get on in the world, to make money, to scale the social ladder, to carve a career for themselves, to blaze their names across the sky of fame. Others are less blatantly egoistic. They are at pains to camouflage their real motives and often make a huge fuss about serving their fellows, cultivating public spirit, discharging one's duty to the state, and so on. But it may be said without cynicism that, quite often, both are at bottom pretty much alike—out for their own ends, with a sharp eye to the main chance, feverishly pursuing, whether avowedly or not, "miserable aims that end with self."

Now, there is nothing more elemental in human nature than self-interest, and doubtless there is a legitimate place for a certain self-concern. We are bidden in the royal law to love our neighbor "as ourselves," the assumption evidently being that some measure of self-love is justifiable and right. As we are preachers, it is our bounden duty to make the most of ourselves for God, and, within the limits of that proviso, it is proper for us to assert ourselves, to provide for ourselves, and to promote our own ends. But it is fatally easy to deceive one's self at this point. It is fatally easy, while making great pretence of serving God, to be really serving oneself all the time.

Speaking candidly, I do not think there is, for serious-minded men, a more critical problem in the ministry than this. I say, "for serious-minded men," because some are too morally insensitive to be so much as aware of a conflict in this connection. But any man to whom his motives vastly matter has here a first-class problem on hand. Not content with simply doing the right thing, he insists on being sure that he is doing it for the right reason. And there the nerve of his trouble lies bare. Brethren, whatever else we are, we must be selfless men! God will make it his business to see to it that we do not achieve much in the ministry if we are not. He has no use for our self-display. I have known ministers—personable, gifted, industrious—possessing, in short, all the qualities and qualifications which seem to promise and to pledge success; and yet they were miserable failures because everything they did was actuated by self-interest, a fact which they could not conceal, however artfully they strove to camouflage it. At all costs we must be selfless men. But how, human nature being what it is, are we to be that unless we undergo a radical inner revolution? That was, in truth, a handsome tribute which F. B. Meyer, who knew him well, paid to D. L. Moody. Describing the great evangelist at the height of his popularity, when the world was ringing with his name, Meyer declared: "It seemed as though he had never heard of himself!" What a compliment to a minister of Christ! Moody had experienced the great change—a change from the selfish to the social.

Thirdly, *it is a change from the temporal to the eternal.* May I state the fact quite frankly? All the best preachers have a breath of eternity about them. They seem, in some sense, like men from another world. They personify everlasting principles and enshrine eternal values. Through much secret commerce with heaven they have attained a radiant serenity, like the peace of the untroubled stars. Their center of gravity has passed from the temporal to the eternal.

Of course, here again we must be mindful to maintain a wise balance. Extremes are always perilous. Who would deny that there is a species of preacher who seems almost too taken up, if that may be, with things eternal—the sort of creature who cloisters himself in his study all week and comes out of it on Sunday, blinking like an owl in the unwonted glare of this common world? I do not say you are to be like him. Presumably, if we were meant to be in eternity at this moment, Providence would have arranged for our transport thither! But no. We are still here; and while we are here, we have a duty in our present sphere.

Yet if, in the words of the well-worn cliché, a minister may be "too heavenly to be of any earthly use," he may also, by the same token, be too earthly to be of any heavenly use. That is, in truth, a terrible state. To be so absorbed in the things of eternity as to neglect the things of time may indeed be deplorable; but to be so preoccupied with the affairs of time as to ignore the vast concerns of eternity is infinitely worse. With that, you may remember, a repentant Chalmers severely taxed himself. Referring to the days when he had deemed it possible and proper to combine the pastoral care of the parish of Kilmany with intense preparation for the Chair of Mathematics in the University of Edinburgh, he publicly confessed: "But what is the object of mathematical science? Magnitudes and the proportions of magnitudes! But in those days I had forgotten two magnitudes. I thought not of the littleness of time, and I recklessly thought not of the greatness of eternity." These are magnitudes which no preacher can afford to forget. The true minister of Christ is a man who has experienced the change from the temporal to the eternal.

There, then, in brief summary, are the preacher's spiritual prerequisites. Fundamentally he is a man who has undergone the great change—a change tranferring the main interests of his life from the sensual to the spiritual, from the selfish to the social, and from the temporal to the eternal.

III

Taking one step further, let us now look at him *in his official capacity*.

To every student of the New Testament it must be staringly plain that it was not Paul's normal practice to set forth his thoughts with formal precision. He wrote under the compulsion of a tumultuous inspiration, not with the tidy orderliness of a passionless logician. Hence, wherever in his writings we come upon a passage which is more than ordinarily systematic, it is a fair inference that the order is of special significance; an inference which is confirmed when the same facts are presented in roughly the same sequence elsewhere in his writings. A noteworthy example of this is to be found in Eph. 4:11, where Paul enumerates the offices in the Christian ministry: "And he [Jesus] gave some, apostles; and some, prophets; and some, evangelists; and some, pastors and teachers." With slight variations, the same catalogue occurs in I Cor. 12, and in both contexts it is introduced in such a way as to leave the reader in no doubt that it has the highest sanctions and represents the divine ideal. There can, I think, be little doubt but that the apostle envisages these functions as being fulfilled by different persons. For our present purpose, however, we shall treat them as facets of preaching in general and thus from various standpoints portraying the preacher in his professional position.

Examing these Pauline passages narrowly, we arrive at the following five conclusions concerning the work of the Christian minister: *as apostle he is to challenge the will; as prophet he is to probe the conscience; as evangelist he is to woo the heart; as pastor he is to care for the soul; as teacher he is to inform the mind.* All these are aspects of the duty of the servant of the Word.

To commence with, *as apostle he is to challenge the will.* The Greek verb *apostello,* of which the English adjective "apostolic" is practically an exact transcription, signified the sending forth of a person by a higher power for a specific purpose. It carried the connotation of authority.

Take up your New Testament and look at Peter and the rest of the apostles as they appear after Pentecost, and is not that precisely the impression which they make upon you? Manifestly these men are under Royal orders; they are acting on a mandate from the Most High; they are conscious that behind them, when they speak, lies all the might of enthroned omnipotence. The boldness which so distinguishes them as they front the hostile magistrates of

Jerusalem is not a mere brute daring: it is the courage of those who know that they represent the Crown.

Nobody with any right to an opinion would dispute that this accent of authority is lamentably lacking in the preaching of today. "We don't blow the loud trumpet nowadays," confessed J. D. Jones; "we tootle on the melancholy flute." The tone of present-day preaching is apt to be diffident, conciliatory, apologetic, when it ought to be confident, challenging, dogmatic. The preacher may enlighten the mind and even touch the heart; but he does not, nearly as often as he should, speak as one who expects to be obeyed. Yet that is plainly part of his duty. As apostle he is to challenge the will.

"But," you may protest, "what has all this got to do with me? I am not in the least like an apostle. Don't talk to me as if I were one of the Twelve. I am only an ordinary individual with very indifferent gifts. If it is to apostles you are addressing yourself, count me out. For I am nothing of the kind." But wait a bit. Were the Twelve, as we call them, after all so very exceptional? Were they really categorically different from ourselves? I do not think so. Personally, I hold that we are all wrong in our common estimate of those primitive apostles. I grant you that two or three of them were outstanding, but what of all the rest? As R. C. Gillies remarks:

> Our Lord did not fill the apostolic college with geniuses. Some geniuses there were—John, with his wonderful mysticism; Peter, the genius of driving-power; Paul, whose life was like a flame, and his mind both penetrative and constructive, poet and theologian in one. But among the Twelve there were also those who contributed nothing to the New Testament. Philip and Andrew never moved a multitude.

The original apostles were men uncommonly like ourselves. Only they had this distinction: they had dwelt much in intimate fellowship with Jesus, and, as a consequence, when they spoke, however humbly and haltingly, behind their utterances rolled the thunders of the eternal throne. May not you and I, by adopting similar means, achieve similar results? To do so is our task. The preacher as apostle should challenge the will.

But, in any case, is not all such argumentation really beside the point? For if Christ be the Burden of our ministry, if he be the content of our preaching, are not our pulpit pronouncements bound to be marked by apostolic authority? After all, he is the "Apostle and High Priest of our profession." With Christ as our theme our words can but challenge the wills of those who hear them.

Again, the preacher *as prophet is to probe the conscience.* There is no note in the entire gamut of the gospel which the preacher of today needs to trumpet forth more loudly than this: "It is not lawful for thee." In every man's ministry there come hours of crisis when, unless he is to be traitorous to the truth and disloyal to duty, he must face evil men as Elijah faced Ahab, as Nathan faced David, as John the Baptist faced Herod, as the personification of the moral law. And such an undertone of crisis ought to run through all his preaching. Nobody cares, of course, to have his conduct thus summarily condemned, and so the prophets are seldom popular among their contemporaries; afterward, however, they are generally appreciated at their true value. As a modern poet, Christopher Morley, has piquantly put it: "Prophets were twice stoned—first, in anger; then, after their death, with a handsome slab in the graveyard." The true preacher must take the risk of this double stoning, even though he is likelier to be accorded the first than the second. But let him take heart. It is amazing how in the long run honest folk come to respect, to revere, and even to love a man who speaks the truth without fear or favor. Very often the prophet is a man with a big stick: we do not like the stick, but we usually in time perceive that the prophet had the right end of it. The preacher as prophet is to probe the conscience.

And here, too, if Christ be the Burden of your ministry, your words are bound to be charged with prophetic power. For is not Christ the supreme Prophet, the Prophet to whom all other true prophets point and from whom they derive their inspiration? Who ever searched the secret places of men's souls as did Jesus? Who ever snatched the mask from the hypocrite's face as did he? Who ever so cut to the moral quick or so ran truth into human hearts like cold steel? Preach Christ, and as Prophet he will probe the consciences of all who hear you.

Once more, *as evangelist the preacher is to woo the heart.* I take it, of course, that the Church must always have professional evangelists, men who specialize in this branch of Christian work and who by aptitude and training are peculiarly fitted for it. The wisdom of this proceeding is amply demonstrated by the success which has attended the labors of such preachers in the past. Think of John Wesley, George Whitefield, Howell Harris, D. L. Moody, John McNeill, and a host of others in that glorious succession. How much they accomplished through a massive concentration on the evangelistic issue! Nevertheless, while there is an undoubted need for such specialized evangelism, we must never suffer ourselves to forget that evangelism is also an integral and inalienable part of the general ministry of the Church. Charles Haddon Spurgeon, Alexander Maclaren, Campbell Morgan—to mention no more!—demonstrated in their own cases past all doubt that it is possible for a preacher to occupy the same pulpit for years, and yet to exercise a mighty evangelistic ministry. That, at present, is our most pressing need. W. B. Sangster puts his finger on the pulse of the matter when he says that the pity is that nowadays evangelism seems so largely to have got into the wrong hands, and that many fine Christians, on whose support of such a project one might confidently have counted, hold off from it all because they do not approve of the methods of certain well-meaning but misguided evangelists, whose technique seems mainly to consist in the exploitation of mass emotion. Yet the prevalence of the spurious ought not to prejudice us against the real, or the presence of the false to lead to the absence of the true.

There is a subtle temptation to which all ministers are subject. It is to regard the frontiers of their own congregations as the limits of their responsibilities. After all, they argue, no man can possibly hope to make much of an impression on the world at large. Far more likely is he to succeed if he deliberately narrows his field of operation and concentrates his powers on a patch of social life whose dimensions are clearly defined, much as a father might without much compunction contemplate the hunger of other people's children, provided his own were well fed. Now that is wrong—criminally wrong! The command of the Master is: "Lift up your eyes, and look on the field." Widen your horizon: broaden the base of your activities; recognize responsibility for those beyond the range of your own religious group. As evangelist the preacher is to seek to woo the world's heart.

For, mark you, this is the big issue now. Beside it all other issues are but side issues. What Christianity supremely needs today is not alone expositors who, with delving minds, seek to plumb its hidden depths and to construct upon them elaborate theological theories—though they have, of course, their proper, honored place. What Christianity needs more than anything else is popularization, dynamic proclamation, the widespread public presentation of its essential message. Are we not far too parochial, even congregational, in our outlook? And do we not need constantly to remind ourselves that Christ died for all, flinging his bleeding arms around the world? Consequently, any minister who takes less than the world for his parish is behaving as though he believed that the Lord's arm were somehow shortened that it could not save.

But here, again, if Christ be the Burden of your ministry, how can your preaching be other than evangelistic in the best sense? Not only is he the Evangelist: he is the Evangel, and there is no better way of wooing the world's heart than by preaching him.

Further, *the preacher as pastor is to care for the soul.* Is it, do you think, a little thing that he who described himself as "the good shepherd" and who declared that it was to be the mark of the good shepherd to give his life for the sheep—is it, I ask, a little thing that he should have applied the same lovely epithet to his unworthy minister? Of all the titles given to the public servant of the Lord none is more tenderly appealing than this—"pastor"—and I cannot conceive of a nobler tribute payable to a minister of Christ than to say that when he comes into people's minds it is naturally and most notably in that capacity that he does so. Some men, of course, have commonly gone by that title, such as John Robinson and Charles Haddon Spurgeon; but I am not thinking about that, although those just named do rank high in the pastoral category. I am thinking rather of men like Samuel Rutherford and Richard Baxter; about them, although they were not known by the title, it is impossible to think at all and the idea of pastorship be far away. It was a saying of Bengel's that "the minister who does not at the same time exercise pastoral work is like a bird with one wing." There may be a great deal of flapping but there is no flight. Those eminent ministers of Christ just mentioned, however, had each two broad pinions on which they bore their people magnificently heavenward. That is the preacher's proud privilege. As pastor he is to care for the soul.

How better can he do that than by making Christ the Burden of his ministry? For Christ, as we have seen, is the great Pastor, who, having long ago given his life *for* the sheep, still gives his life *to* the sheep wherever he is faithfully presented.

Finally, *the preacher as teacher is to inform the mind.* Preaching and teaching, it is to be noted, are not by any means the same. The former is personal, occasional, sporadic: the latter is general, formal, systematic. While, however, teaching is not preaching, preaching is, in a sense, teaching, since the generic includes the specific although the specific does not comprehend the generic. There is a type of teaching, to be sure, which is not preaching at all. It is separated by a whole diameter from that warm spate of spirited speech which, in real preaching, gushes straight from the heart. Such teaching is the cold, dispassionate discussion of doctrine, a kind of homiletical autopsy in which analysis may disclose the parts of truth but cannot infuse into them the fire of life. That sort of dialectic doubtless has a place in the Christian Church. But it is not with that that we are here directly concerned: it is rather with the didactic element implicit in all true preaching itself. In this sense the preacher as teacher must inform the mind.

Now, to any thinking person, a moment's reflection must serve to show that if, in his ministry, a man is mediating to the world the everlasting Jesus, then, whatever else he may or may not be doing, he is at any rate communicating to them the greatest moral Teacher in the history of mankind. That is a stupendous bestowal, and surely it is what Paul had in mind when he wrote: "Ye need not that I write unto you: for ye yourselves are taught of God." Thus to convey to men's hearts the eternal Jesus, furnishing them, so to say, with an interior Tutor, is infinitely more for their moral profiting than wagon loads of ethical instruction and exhortation. To transmit Christ in this way is the preacher's high prerogative and holy task. By communicating Christ as Teacher he is to inform the mind.

CHAPTER THREE

THE CRAFT

IN AN INTIMATE STUDY of Alexander Maclaren, the great expositor of Manchester, there is an exquisite piece of portraiture in which he appears as a young man applying himself assiduously to the craft of sermon composition. It is a picture which appeals strongly to the imagination. Rummaging about among the lumber in an attic of the house in which he then lived, he came upon a military cloak, a helmet, and an old sword, evidently heirlooms in the family. And, when he sat down at his desk as a theological student, he was wont to put on the cloak and the helmet and to lay the sword by his side as he addressed himself to the work.

You are not likely to make much headway in homiletical craftsmanship save as you set about it in a like militant spirit. The art is so dauntingly difficult and proficiency in it so hard to acquire that unless you bring to it a stout heart and a stubborn resolve, God helping you, to see the thing through, you will probably be tempted ere long to throw it up and to turn to tasks more congenial and yielding more rapid returns. That, however, would be a tragedy; for there is no work in the world which better deserves doing or which deserves doing better than that of mediating the Word of God.

There is, indeed, a species of sermon whose construction calls for no special skill. The thing can be done almost in one's sleep. Mind you: I am not saying anything about the result! It may be a rushing spate of turgid rhetoric, or it may be the sort of joinered article of which John Watson somewhere says that it can be "knocked together with a few bits of wood and a pot of glue." In any case it will not be the kind of sermon you would find any satisfaction in preaching. And, incidentally, in this connection, may I urge you to cultivate what may be called a homiletical conscience, making it morally impossible for you to compose or to deliver a discourse unworthy of your powers? Yet surely there is scant need for such an admonition; for if you love the work, you will scorn to scamp it and will want to put into it the best you can. Nor is there anything of either pleasure or profit, for preacher or hearers, in a shoddy, jerry-built address.

Granted, then, that you are ready to grapple with your great task, assuming that you have soaked your mind in scripture and purged your heart by prayer, how are you to start with the actual work of making the sermon? This is the subject now before us, and it is one which merits and will handsomely repay the closest heed.

Proceeding on the Aristotelian principles, let us begin at the beginning. Obviously, the first thing to do is to choose a text. Exceptional occasions there may be when you will not require to do this. In days of revival, for instance, when the arm of the Lord is made redeemingly bare, you may be able to dispense with the practice altogether. So at least Howell Harris found under such conditions. "I took no particular texts," he records, "but discoursed freely as the Lord gave me utterance." At times, too, you will be spared the trouble of tracking texts: they instead will track you. Spurgeon in one place speaks about scriptural passages which, he says, leap out upon the preacher, like a lion from a thicket, demanding to be dealt with. In such circumstances you will be saved the search for a suitable verse. Plainly, however, such propitious hours will be the exceptions rather than the rule, and generally you will find it requisite diligently to dig about in the Word of God for passages adapted to sermonic treatment. The advantages of the time-honored custom of taking a text are manifold and manifest: a text tethers a man to the Bible, a text keeps him to the point, a text imparts to his pulpit utterances a majesty and an authority of which they would otherwise be destitute, and so on. Besides, if you do not employ a text, the probability is that you will produce not a sermon but an essay; and instead of propagating divine truth, you will only ventilate your own views. Hence, in your preaching, always start from a stated verse or passage of the Holy Book.

On this topic there are several counsels I would tender. To start with, let me urge you to select *striking and suggestive texts*, texts which stir and stimulate the mind. It cannot honestly be said that all texts possess this quality. William Austin, who flourished in the reign of James I, preached once from the words: "And Bartholomew." History has not judged it necessary to preserve anything of what he said! Sydney Smith, the clerical humorist, is reported to have actually committed himself to the opinion that any sequence of scripture words or sentences whatsoever would serve as text for a sermon, and to have seriously proposed to a ministerial friend the following: "Parthians, and Medes, and Elamites, and the dwellers in Mesopotamia." That scarcely seems a very promising passage. (Personally, I would as soon try to preach on the multiplication table!) It would be interesting to know what Smith himself could have made of it! Choose, then, texts with a tongue in their heads, texts that have hands to grip you and legs to walk straight into your hearers' hearts.

By this I do not mean that you are to choose *outré*, odd, out-of-the-way texts. Behind the selection of such there are two possible motives: one, a desire on the part of the preacher to call public attention to his exegetical cleverness or at least to what he fancies himself to possess in that direction; the other, to impart freshness and vividness to the truth. In the first case, the choice is strongly to be deprecated; in the second, there may be something to be said for it. At all events, this is very clear: once let a congregation be thoroughly convinced of a preacher's loyalty to the focal facts of the faith and its members will not greatly mind what texts or passages he selects as subjects for his sermons, queer and quaint though they may sometimes seem, because they will know intuitively that, however far a compass he may fetch, it will not be long till he is heading to Christ. This explains why such a man as Spurgeon was able, without offending the sensibilities or alienating the sympathies of his vast audiences, to preach on such curious questions as, "Is there any taste in the white of an egg?" and why Talmage found it possible to get away with a sermon on so miscellaneous a mystery as this: "The owl, vulture, bat, chameleon, and snail." Such preachers could be trusted to be loyal to the truth. Their people knew instinctively that, in choosing strange texts, they were not actuated by a vain desire to display their dialectical dexterity but simply to shed fresh light on a familiar theme. If, however, on the other hand, the preacher's hearers do *not* have this conviction concerning their minister, they are in peril of passing very swift judgment upon him and of setting him down out of hand as a mountebank and a fool.

Occasionally, I suspect, you will feel that a sermon is imprisoned in a particular text and you will long to set it at liberty. Nor is there anything quite so tantalizing and exasperating as trying key after key in a vain endeavor to unlock the dungeon door. But be of good heart. When God's time comes for you to preach on it, he will send his angel and bring it forth. I would warn you, however, not to waste precious hours meantime in a futile effort to pick the lock!

Sometimes, to be sure, texts and topics will suggest themselves to you in the strangest ways. Everybody knows, for instance, how the idea worked out in his great sermon on "The Expulsive Power of a New Affection" came to Chalmers in a carriage when, in conversation with the coachman, he heard him say that, whenever his horse came to a dangerous bend in the road where it was apt to take fright, he gave it a flick with his whip to furnish it with something else to think about. Of similar point is the tale of how, when Spurgeon lived at Cambridge, he was unable on one occasion to find a text for his evening sermon in a certain village. Try as he might the right verse would not come. Presently, walking to a window in his home, he saw on the roof of the house opposite, a crowd of sparrows pecking the life out of an escaped canary. Instantly the words of Jer. 12:9 leaped into his mind: "Mine heritage is unto me as a speckled bird, the birds round about her are against her." Spurgeon had his sermon. Proceeding to his appointment with great composure, he preached most powerfully on: "The Peculiar People and the Persecution of Their Enemies." When such circumstances set a text at liberty, the hour has come to preach on it; but until the angel of release arrives, you will probably find the four quaternions of soldiers more than a match for you!

However that may be, the cardinal principle governing your selection of a text must ever be that *it is such as may be made a vehicle for the transmission of the everlasting Christ.* Nothing matters more; for if the passage you select for homiletic treatment cannot carry Christ, if it cannot be employed as a medium for the transmission of the eternal Word, you must cast it aside as insufficient for your purpose. After all, you cannot reasonably hope to offer Christ effectively to your people if you take as texts meatless morsels with no evangelical relevance or appeal. Try preaching on Gideon's trumpet or on Ezra's nine-and-twenty knives, and then preach on John 3:16 or Gal. 2:20, and note the difference. The former may provide you with a platform for the demonstration of your homiletical ingenuity: the latter will give you an opportunity to proclaim the unsearchable riches of Christ. Never forget that no preacher has pinions who has only opinions, but that he who has Christ for his theme has wings on his words. Taking some fancy topic, you will probably find that you are left to work the things out as best you can with your own unaided powers: taking a great evangelical text, you may confidently count on the inward reinforcement of the Holy Ghost. Not all texts, of course, are equally serviceable in this direction. Some convey Christ to us to once: others are like roads, long or short, straight or tortuous, by which he comes to us. Choose texts that mediate the Master.

Before passing from this front-rank subject, I should like to raise one or two further points with reference to the length of texts. That will, to be sure, vary from time to time in accordance with the type of treatment on which you decide and also in relation to the structure of the text itself. Now and then you will take a bare word. In that case it will have to be a rich and lustrous word, a coruscating jewel of suggestive thought. In your preaching you will lay hold of that jewel and lift it up before the people, turning it first this way and then that, so that each brilliant facet will catch and reflect its rays, and you will go on doing this until, for your hearers, the word shall come to have a burning beauty it never had before. Richard Waugh has done this in masterly manner with the word "departure" as it occurs in II Tim. 4:6: "The time of my *departure* is at hand." Taking the Greek term *analusis,* of which "departure" is the English translation, he examines its various significations in the colloquial Greek of the period in which the New Testament was written, and of these he makes four memorable points: (1) *It was a seaman's word*, used of the "unloosing" of a ship from its anchorage; (2) *It was a plowman's term,* denoting the "unyoking" of a weary team of horses after a toilsome day; (3) *It was a traveler's expression,* suggesting the "striking of a tent," preparatory to setting out on a march; (4) *It was a philosopher's term,* signifying the "solution of a problem." There, within the compass of a single word, you have compressed a wealth of instructive and illuminative thought. Sometimes you will take as text but one word.

More often, though, you will probably select a phrase or sentence or even a longer passage of scripture. Do not let it be too long, however, or you will find it difficult, in dealing with it in an expository fashion, to maintain a just balance in your handling of its component parts and you will be tempted, because of the pressure of time, to turn a blind eye to some of its aspects or, for lack of artistic judgment, to make too much of others. Yet do not, on the other hand, generally speaking, let it be too short either, or you may find it necessary to go too far afield in search of material to pad the sermon out to its proper proportions. As a general rule do not select as subject a passage containing more than three or at the most four complete clauses. Under normal circumstances you will probably discover that this is as much as you can comfortably manage in any one message.

You might care to take what I may term "twin texts" on occasion. The practice is particularly rewarding. Pick out two small passages of scripture because you perceive that there is a logical bond between them and bracket them together either for purposes of contrast or comparison. It cannot have escaped you that some texts seem almost to have been made for one another, although perhaps widely separated so far as their biblical locations are concerned. They fit one another as the hand fits the glove, as the bee the flower. Take these two descriptions of the divine dealings with the Hebrew people: "As a hen gathereth" (Matt. 23:37) and "As an eagle stirreth up" (Deut. 32:11). Or take this textual couplet which is fraught with homiletical suggestiveness: "And David went up by the ascent of mount Olivet, and wept as he went up, and had his head covered, and he went barefoot: and all the people that was with him covered every man his head, and they went up weeping" (II Sam. 15:30); and, "When he was come nigh, even now at the descent of the mount of Olives, the whole multitude of the disciples began to rejoice and praise God with a loud voice for all the mighty works that they had seen; saying, Blessed be the King that cometh in the name of the Lord: peace in heaven, and glory in the highest. . . . And when he was come near, he beheld the city, and wept over it" (Luke 19:37-38, 41). Or, perhaps most striking of all, take the two stories of the prodigal son—that in the Old Testament and that in the New. You will find the former in Deut. 21:18-21 and the latter, of course, in Luke 15:11-32. Occasionally, then, you will preach on two texts or passages.

More popular still is the practice of taking three. There seems to be a rule of three running through the Bible, and you would do well, in selecting passages for preaching purposes, to avail yourselves of whatever assistance this affords. May I submit a few samples of such arresting textual trilogies? Here is one: "Where is the lamb?" (Gen. 22:7); "Behold the Lamb" (John 1:29); "Worthy is the Lamb" (Rev. 5:12). The man who does not warm to that marvelous sequence was never meant to be a preacher. And here is a further trilogy which supplies us with a threefold answer to the question as to why Christ died: "Christ died for our sins" (I Cor. 15:3); "Christ died for us" (Rom. 5:8); "Christ died that he might be Lord" (Rom. 14:9). As a final example consider the three occasions upon which Paul asserts the sublime universality of the gospel and the reason which, in each case, he assigns for this: "There is no difference between the Jew and the Greek: *for the same Lord over all is rich unto all that call upon him*" (Rom. 10:12); "There is neither Jew nor Greek, there is neither bond nor free, there is neither male nor female: *for ye are all one in Christ Jesus*" (Gal. 3:28); "There is neither Greek nor Jew, circumcision nor uncircumcision, Barbarian, Scythian, bond nor free: *but Christ is all, and in all*" (Col. 3:11). To anybody with the least trace of homiletical imagination it must be thrillingly obvious that simply to string such texts together is to go a long way toward producing a telling sermon.

Having, then, chosen your text, study it closely. Consult the original, examine the various modern versions, read the context several times and observe in what ways that modifies it and how it conditions its application. In short make absolutely sure that, in tackling the text, you know precisely what you are about. I stress this because otherwise you may find to your infinite annoyance that, after spending much precious time in the exegesis and analysis of a verse, you have mistaken its proper meaning and so put yourself to profound trouble to no purpose. Be certain, therefore, before attempting to expound your text, that you know exactly what it means.

After this should come a period of incubation. Do not avidly get to grips with your text as soon as you have decided upon it. Let it simmer in your brain for a while. "By what law of the mind is it," asks Harriet Beecher Stowe, "that an idea, long overlooked and trodden underfoot as a useless stone, suddenly sparkles out in new light as a discovered diamond?" On the value of this meditating on the text the great preachers speak with one voice. "I like to lie and soak in my text," says Spurgeon. "I sometimes think," observes Maclaren, "that a verse in the Psalms carries the whole pith of homiletics: "While I was musing the fire burned, then spake I with my tongue." "It is when the subject has been long tossed about in thought," states Salker, "that the mind begins to glow about it; the subject itself gets hot and begins to melt and flash, until at last it can be poured out in a facile and glowing stream." Wherefore, never attempt to tackle a text when it is "cold": wait till it begins to flash and flame. This will happen as you prayerfully hold it in your mind and heart for a while; and, remember, the quality of the expression which you ultimately give to it will be exactly proportionate to the depth and extent of its impression upon you. Weigh the text well, therefore, before setting to work on it.

The true preacher is always with child of a sermon. No sooner has he delivered one than he is fecund of another. Homiletically he does not live from hand to mouth, preparing each address for some precise occasion and meeting each sermonic emergency as it arises. Always he is bearing a living Burden—the Burden of the Lord. This may not seem, in the abstract, a very attractive prospect. It may cause the preacher's life to appear one of intolerable strain, interminable tension, an existence ever striving to express something beyond itself and always conscious of paralyzing frustration because unable fully to do so. But that is a false idea. Actually the true preacher finds delight in this perpetual homiletical pregnancy. Sometimes you will hear him singing a Magnificat, and then you will know he has conceived a new message. "We come," says Coquerel, "to take a sincere pleasure in this unbroken tension of mind as it works for the pulpit." Study, then, not for stated occasions only, when you have a definite demanding appointment in view: study all the time, every available moment, every eligible hour. Always be in travail of the truth.

Arrived at this stage, you are in a way to start with the actual treatment of your text. The first thing to be done, as J. H. Jowett discerningly insisted, is to try to find a crisp crystallizing phrase, precisely pat to the point in hand and covering as far as possible every aspect of the topic with which you propose to deal. This terse and luminous sentence may serve, if need be, as the advertised title of your discourse. You may actually use it as such, or you may not. Whatever you do, see that you *can* thus succinctly express your theme in a clear-cut clause. If you cannot, the presumption is that you are not really ready to begin and will require to give fuller consideration to the matter before getting down to the treatment of it. Sum up your subject. That is the first law of successful composition, a law the advantages of conformity to which are clear to everyone who sits down to think about it. Its rewards are multifarious. It helps to focus your thinking on the topic under review and prevents you from mentally wandering off in pursuit of illusive will-o'-the-wisps which, promising to lead you aright, land you at last, if you follow them, in logical quagmires. And, by the way, should you decide to advertise your subject, there are two pitfalls to be avoided. One is that of making the title so insufferably dull or pitifully naïve as to be incapable of stirring the most tepid interest or even so much as arresting attention at all. I recollect seeing once on the notice board of a city church the minister's sermon title for the following Sunday. Apparently it was one of a series under the general heading "The Religious Message of Nursery Rhymes," and I was intrigued to discover (or was I?) that the topic next to be treated was: "Little Miss Muffet"! Do not let your title be trite or tame. But, equally, do not fly to the opposite extreme in search of the melodramatic and sensational and forget the proprieties of the occasion after the fashion of a preacher I once knew who took as text a brief prayer from Isaiah, "Undertake for me," and gave out as topic: "Send for the Undertaker!" Preserve the happy medium. Make your title as striking and even startling as may be. But have a sacred care, in your concern to secure a hearing, not to violate the canons of good taste.

As examples of arresting and expressive sermon titles may I adduce the following? On the text "He made as though he would have gone further" (Luke 24:28), F. W. Boreham has a thoughtful address under the inspired heading: "The Illusion of Divine Indifference." To a sermon on the moral leadership of Jesus, Reinhold Niebuhr has given the unforgettable title: "The Relevance of an Impossible Ideal." While the phrase by which D. E. Bryan indicates the content of a discourse on one part of the parable of the prodigal son is: "The High Cost of Low Living." Not always, of course, will you be able to hit so happily on a form of words which matches and focuses your theme so finely; but you must not on that account excuse yourself from making the effort. Never begin work on a sermon until you have hammered out some such vivid summary of the truth it is meant to convey and found a heading which exactly expresses it; for such a title serves the twofold purpose of clarifying your own thought when writing the sermon and of rendering it more rememberable to those who afterward hear it.

At this point we have reached a position from which we are able to make a total survey of our theme; we have a map of it, so to speak, before our mind's eye, and we can now visualize it as a whole and see the relation of part to part. We are, therefore, ready to determine to which type of treatment it is likely to be most amenable, and how accordingly it were best to tackle it.

Broadly speaking, there are, of course, two ways in which you may do so. Technically they are known respectively as the topical and the expository, the synthetic and the analytic. Perhaps if we use figurative language the matter will become plainer. The first method, then, may be called the "magnet" or the "snowball" method. And that for this reason. Setting the text in the center of your mind, as a sort of magnet, a focus of fascination, you allow it to gather round itself all relevant or related data, drawing upon memory's ample stores and laying under tribute everything germane in the treasury of your consciousness. Or, to express the same thing otherwise, the text is like a snowball, rolling backward and forward in your thought and growing more and more in bulk as it goes until at last it reaches the requisite dimensions. The other method—the expository—consists, on the contrary, in performing a sort of autopsy on the text, laying it, as it were, on the dissecting table and, with the deft application of the homiletical scalpel, taking it to pieces and then stitching it up again. (Remember, however, in this connection the sad fate of Humpty Dumpty!) Both methods are valid and valuable, and it is for you to make up your mind in each case which is the fitter to serve your immediate purpose.

All this leads us to the vital matter of drawing up an outline. Here, as I have said, the nature of the plan you propose to produce will be determined by the type of treatment on which you have resolved. If you intend to treat the text topically, the heads will naturally correspond with the logical divisions of your subject; whereas, if you purpose handling it in an expository way, your points will simply be the names you affix to the various sections into which you dissect your text.

Not all texts, to be sure, nor all subjects, can be carved up in the same manner. As an old preacher shrewdly observes,

> Sometimes the words naturally fall asunder, sometimes they melt, sometimes they untwist, and there be some words so willing to be parted that

they divide themselves, to the great ease and rejoicing of the minister. But if they will not easily come to pieces, then he falls to hacking and hewing, as if he would make all fly to shivers. The truth of it is: I have known, now and then, some knotty texts that have been divided seven or eight times over before they could make them split handsomely according to their mind.

Do not, nevertheless, permit the seeming preachability of a text or subject, its apparent amenableness to sermonic analysis, to betray you into dealing with it naïvely, merely accentuating the main words or basic ideas, chopping the passage or topic up into little bits and talking about each in turn. You may recall the humorous burlesque of the sermon of a once-famous London preacher. The sermon is supposed to have been on "Old Mother Hubbard" and the treatment as follows: "First, my friends, she was old; next, she was a mother; again, she loved her dog, and so on." Beware of descending to such bathos and banality. Truly the Lord preserveth the simple, but this is a simplicity from which a preacher might well pray to be preserved. Genuine simplicity never comes from paucity of thought or from intellectual infantilism, but always from clarity of conception and lucidity of expression. That sort of simplicity is a prime prerequisite to effective preaching. Need I urge you not to copy the profound divine who is reported to have preached before a rural congregation a sermon whose points I subjoin: (1) *Pleromatic Humanity;* (2) *Pleromatic Divinity;* (3) *Hypostatical Union*? By all means state your texts strikingly, but whom in all the world are they likely to strike if they go whizzing over people's heads? You have perhaps heard of W. L. Watkinson's witty retort when charged with preaching over the heads of his congregation: "Brethren, lift up your heads!" But there is a limit beyond which common folk are incapable of such capital elevation. They are not trained theologians, most of them, nor are they conversant with the jargon of the schools. Wherefore, moderate the thought in your messages to meet their mental capacity. It is of no use speaking to them if they do not understand you.

Perhaps this will be as proper a place as any at which to insert a few remarks on the matter of serial preaching. Some subjects, it is plain, are too big to be adequately treated in one sermon. You cannot hope to do anything like justice to a whole book of the Bible, for instance, within the limits of a single address. Nor can you reasonably expect to deal exhaustively with some great Christian doctrine and its correlatives and corollaries in a solitary discourse. For this reason you will at times preach connected series of sermons on stated themes, taking first one aspect of the subject and then another, and thus maintaining the balance of truth and helping your hearers toward a total view of things. Here again, however, let your moderation be known unto all men. Nothing is likelier to scatter a congregation to the four winds than a protracted series of sermons on some dull and tedious topic. Variety is the spice of homiletics. Of Joseph Caryl, an old Puritan, Spurgeon tells that he lectured Sunday after Sunday for seven years on the book of Job, starting with five hundred auditors and finishing with five—faint yet pursuing! Origen, the ancient Church father, is said to have produced the same effect by preaching his twenty-two sermons on Ps. 119. Even the homiletical genius of Alexander Whyte was severely taxed, as Gossip has hinted, by his four years' course on the subject of prayer. That was, to be sure, carrying things too far. Yet, provided you do not unduly extend the series, you may find it profitable on occasion to preach serially. A good series may be prepared on the parables of the Old Testament—the story of the trees choosing a king, Nathan's barbed little tale about the man with the one ewe lamb, Jeremiah's figure of the vineyard, and so on. Another series might be composed on what may be termed "The Unofficial Beatitudes of the Bible": "Blessed is he whose transgression is forgiven, whose sin is covered" (Ps. 32:1); "Blessed are they who keep his testimonies, and that seek him with the whole heart" (Ps. 119:2); "Blessed is he, whosoever shall not be offended in me" (Matt. 11:6). E. C. Comfort has a series of sermons on a striking and stimulating theme, which he entitles, not very happily, "The Partiality of Jesus." The line of thought is an original and unconventional one—Christ's favorite persons and things and places—and the subjects dealt with include: "His Favorite Friend—the Sinner"; "His Favorite Book—Deuteronomy"; "His Favorite Name for Himself—Son of Man"; "His Favorite Title for God—'My Father' "; "His Favorite Place—the Mount of Olives," and the like. As subjects for a sequence of sermons at Christmastide, Andrew Blackwood makes the following attractive suggestion. He proposes that the title be: "The Songs of Our Saviour's Birth," and that the preacher deal in succession with the Magnificat, the Benedictus, the Gloria in Excelsis, and the Nunc Dimittis.

It takes a skillful preacher to run a lengthy series with success. Normally you will find, I think, that four, or at the most five, such discourses are as many as should be dealt with in an unbroken chain. You might some time consider composing a course on "The Christian Paradoxes," limiting the number of addresses to four and giving them respectively the following titles: (1) *The Paradoxes of the Risen Christ,* where your points might be: he is divine and yet human; he is absent and yet present; he is objectively real and yet subjectively receivable. (2) *The Paradoxes of Prayer,* and here your headings might perhaps take such a form as this: the paradox of divine omniscience and human appeal; the paradox of divine omnipotence and human co-operation; the paradox of divine willingness and human importunity. (3) *The Paradoxes of Christian Living,* for which you might take as text Paul's dilemma "I am in a strait betwixt two" (Phil. 1:23) and show how the apostle was torn by the tension between the different worlds in which he was living: the world behind and the world before; the world beneath and the world above; the world within and the world without. And (4) *The Paradoxes of the Kingdom of God,* where the sectional captions might be something like this: it is present and yet future; it is inward; it comes downward and yet must be built upward.

Here let me introduce a few remarks upon the matter of preaching on the great festivals of the Christian year, "revolving the scroll of the Word," as R. F. Horton beautifully puts it, "with the seasons of the rolling year." This is a practice which I unreservedly recommend. In doing so, of course, I do not mean to imply that you are to limit your treatment of the mighty themes of the gospel—the incarnation, the Atonement, the Resurrection, the Ascension, Pentecost—to the dates at which they are officially commemorated. Constantly, in your ministry, you will take occasion to treat of these tremendous topics. But you will probably find, as many another has done, that to deal with such facts at the anniversaries of their occurrence, or at the time of year popularly set apart for their official commemoration, helps to italicize their relevance in people's minds and to maintain the balance of truth in your preaching.

Moving on now to the actual detailed working out of your discourse, we come to the crucial question of the opening paragraph. Few things matter more in a sermon than the manner in which it "takes off." T. M. Lindsay indeed once declared that it did not much signify how you began, since everybody was willing to listen to you for at least a little. But that was surely a false judgment. The introduction is of paramount importance. Moody, to be sure, advised us to pack into the first paragraph all the best things in our message in the hope of thus early gripping our hearers' interest and holding it to the end. That, however, was taking things too far. Still, he was absolutely right in insisting that we must seize the attention of our listeners as soon as ever we can. Aim at a strong and striking start.

This is not a plea for oddness in the sermon opening. There is a singular story about Philip Jones, Porthcawl, a picturesque personality of the Welsh pulpit, who got up once before a great congregation and gave out as text these stout and stirring words, once hurled in defiance by three Hebrew youths at an Oriental despot: "We are not careful to answer thee in this matter." Slowly and deliberately the preacher closed his Bible, took off his glasses, and leisurely polished them with his handkerchief; then, leaping into sudden life, he darted a glance at the people and demanded: "What matter?" A further pause followed, during which he stared at the pulpit floor and fumbled with the folds of his gown. Then, lifting his head like a lion, into the breathless silence he thundered: "The matter that matters!"

Now I have no doubt that electrified the audience, but I cannot, all the same, unreservedly recommend it as an example for you to copy. It was too self-conscious, melodramatic, sensational. After all, there is no special virtue in creating a sensation. On certain conditions anybody can do that. As someone has said, you may enter the pulpit Sunday after Sunday and preach the most eloquent and impassioned sermons and hardly a soul will take any notice of you, but get into the same pulpit and put up an umbrella and next morning the newspapers will be full of it. Be dramatic, if you will, but not melodramatic; gripping, but not at the price of gravity and decorum.

Various modes of opening the sermon may now be briefly viewed and reviewed. There is, first, the classic method, for which a good deal may still be said—that of tracing the text back to its context and starting by examining it in relation to its literary and historical setting. This, by and large, is a capital plan. Just as the airplane taxis along the runway prior to taking off, so the old preachers, before spreading their wings in the treatment of a text, were wont to begin far back, so to speak, gaining speed and gathering momentum for their homiletical ascent by commencing with a sort of running commentary on the scriptural setting of the passage of which they were treating. In this way the text obviously stands a better chance of honest handling, but also it often shines in a new light and gleams with a fresh luster when thus linked to its biblical background.

Take an example. We will suppose that you purpose preaching on these sublime words from the swansong of Moses recorded in Deut. 33:27: "Underneath are the everlasting arms." How immensely more moving and meaningful does the phrase become when looked at in the light of the circumstances amid which it was spoken and out of which it sprang! To throw this into the boldest possible relief your sermon might begin something like this:

For many years Moses had been the strong man in Israel. Metaphorically, he had carried the nation in his arms. His moral muscles had held it firmly together and his iron grasp had kept it from going to pieces during the testing time in the desert. And now the hour had come for him to take a long last leave of the people he loved. He was about to wend his slow way up the steep slope to where in a quiet fold among the hills he was to be laid to rest. His integrating grasp on the nation's affairs was to be relaxed. His lifting leadership was to end. His succoring arms were to be withdrawn. But, ere he took his road, there was one comforting word which he had to say to those to whom he was bidding a final farewell, one solacing sentence with which he sought to still and to strengthen their hearts—"Underneath are the *everlasting* arms."

It will be seen at a glance how luminously alive this great text becomes when treated thus in conjunction with its actual setting in biblical history.

Another mode of beginning is to lead off with a proposition. Stating as starkly and as startlingly as possible at the start the point you mean to make, you proceed to elaborate it throughout your opening paragraph. You are preaching, we will imagine, on the words "He shall see his seed," applied in Isa. 53:10 to the suffering servant of the Lord and which you may warrantably appropriate to Jesus Christ. Commencing with a pithy and expressive statement, you go on to expand it into a short exordium:

Jesus founded no family. In this he differed from most of the great moral teachers of mankind. They were nearly all married men. Confucius, the sage of ancient China, was wed at nineteen. Buddha had a wife and child, though he left both on the day of the baby's birth to begin the religious quest. Mohammed was a father and permitted each of his male followers a maximum of four wives. But Jesus founded no family: he produced no progeny: he engendered no offspring. And when he died, as a modern poet has graphically put it, "without a grey hair in his head," he left no issue behind. In biblical phrase "he did not see his seed."

Yet here is this old Hebrew prophet saying something that seems flatly to contradict that. "He *shall* see his seed," he declares. What are we to make of this?

There a historical fact is stated crisply and clearly, contrasts cited, and a problem presented for solution in the sermon. You may find it profitable on occasion to commence with a proposition.

A third option confronts you in opening your sermon: you may start with a story. This mode of beginning is immensely popular now, and not without good reason, for there is nothing which so gains and grips the interest of an audience as a well-told tale. In searching for a suitable narrative to form the frontispiece of your discourse, you will find that many tracts of human experience may be laid under tribute. A story may strike you in your general reading, or somebody may tell it to you in the course of conversation, or it may be an incident in your personal life. However you happen upon it, see that it is strictly relevant to the subject on hand. Otherwise, it may be like the Marble Arch in London —a magnificent entrance to nowhere! Let the story lead your people straight to the point to which you want to bring them. If it has thrust and punch, and if you know your business in "putting it across," I promise you first-class results from starting with a story.

Here is an example from a recent autobiography which can be made admirably to serve a homiletic purpose. You are dealing, we will assume, with the earthly life of Jesus, holding up before the imagination of your hearers his matchless moral example, and reminding them how its holy perfection thrice called forth from the heavens a commendatory verdict. How better can you introduce the theme than by some such lively and up-to-date allusion as this?

In that racy and eminently readable book *Recollections*, by P. Carnegie Simpson, he tells how once in a hotel in Norway, his wife, a Danish lady with a superb voice, was singing a song by Grieg, the Norwegian composer, when suddenly the door of the apartment was flung open and in burst Grieg himself with the cry—"That is how my songs should be sung!"

You may then go on to make the application as follows:

Three times in the gospels is it recorded that Almighty God did something of that sort during the historic life of Jesus. He broke in, so to speak, thrice on Christ's career—at the Baptism, on the Mount of Transfiguration, and in the court of the temple at Jerusalem—to pronounce a laudatory judgment on the character of his Son. As much as to say—"This is how life should be lived."

Or here is an incident from English history with which you may profitably preface a sermon. You are preaching, it may be, on Paul's categorical outburst in I Cor. 3:21: "All things are yours." (The Christian alternative, by the way, to the Communist doctrine of collective ownership!) And, as you muse on the matter, a vivid scene from England's storied past all at once flashes on to the screen of your mind. Immediately you perceive its amazing appositeness to the topic of which you are treating, and gradually the initial paragraph of your sermon shapes itself like this in your thought:

There is a stirring story—whether fact or fiction, who can tell?—which describes how, when William, duke of Normandy, landed in 1066 at Pevensey on the Sussex coast, a trifling mishap befell him which was very differently interpreted by the intrepid warrior himself, and by his credulous vacillating followers. Leaping ashore from the ship, he missed his footing and fell full-length on the beach, clutching instinctively at the sand with both hands. "An evil omen!" cried his superstitious men. "No," countered the redoubtable Conqueror, "I have taken possession of this land with my two hands. All that is here is ours!"

It requires no great exercise of the imaginative faculty to realize how finely such a narrative may be pressed into service of the text: "All things are yours."

Or, again, let me adduce a further instance of the same sort, based this time on personal observation and recollection. You might want to preach sometime on "The Uplifted Christ," a truly noble theme, and the subject will open up best for you if you consider it in relation to the three great texts in John's Gospel in which Jesus alludes expressly and in set terms to his own elevation on the cross: "When ye shall have lifted up the Son of man, then shall ye know that I am he"; "And as Moses lifted up the serpent in the wilderness, even so must the Son of man be lifted up"; "And I, if I be lifted up from the earth, will draw all men unto me." At the start you may strike your keynote with some such introductory sentences as these:

It is the common custom of the race to uplift its great men. Those who have conspicuously distinguished themselves in one or other of the branches of human thought and action—science, art, literature, statesmanship, and the like—are generally accorded after their death some sort of sculptured elevation. Thus, for example, London has striven to show its unbounded admiration for Horatio Nelson by placing a stone statue of him on top of a colossal column in Trafalgar Square. Glasgow, in its civic center, has given a like eminence to Sir Walter Scott. While Hull, in its turn, has bestowed on William Wilberforce a similar pillared prominence.

Now, nigh on twenty centuries ago, there came into history One who, measured by merely human standards, was immeasurably greater than any other in the long record of the race. On the principle which we have just illustrated one would expect that to him would be accorded an elevation higher than that conferred upon any other. We should anticipate that he would be not only eminent but pre-eminent. We would look to find the world uplifting him. And so it did! He was uplifted! But how differently from the manner he merited!

Thus in less than two hundred words you have done a couple of workmanlike things: gripped the interest of your hearers and blazed a trail right to the heart of your subject. What more is an introduction designed to do?

Yet another mode of launching an address you may usefully employ. You may begin with a question. Subscribing to the dictum of Socrates, you may hold that the finest way of making room in people's minds for the truth you wish to impart is not to try to drive it into them with a sledge hammer but rather to elicit their assent to it by causing them to discover it for themselves. Hence, start with a plain and pointed inquiry, and thus set your listeners moving, so to say, "under their own steam" along the lines on which you intend later to travel, thus clearing the track for your own train of thought. As an example I offer the following exordium from a sermon on "The Centrality of Christ":

> What is your life's real center? What is the pivot round which it revolves, the focal point about which it organizes itself? With some, it is pleasure; with some, it is personal ambition; with some, it is the accumulation of wealth; with some, it is the quest for truth; with some, it is the passionate love of beauty; with some, it is a commandingly creative task. But, whatever it may be, it is, for the individual concerned, the spindle, so to speak, round which the whole of life rotates.

In this introduction you stab your congregation broad awake at one stroke with a startling query and, keeping them morally on the *qui vive* by making it plain that you are dealing with a live, practical issue, expose the folly of giving first place in one's affections to anybody or to anything other than Christ, and thus pave the way for your main contention that life finds its true centrality in Jesus.

One further mode of opening remains—that of beginning with a catching quotation. Let me illustrate. You are taking as topic, we will say, the phrase "desperate men," and you tether your discourse to Matt. 11:12: "The kingdom of heaven suffereth violence, and the violent take it by force." How better can you preface it than with these gripping words of Karl Barth: "We do not rightly read the Bible until we read it like desperate men"? Or perhaps your theme is Jesus and the Resurrection, and you found your sermon on Paul's somber supposition in I Cor. 15:14: "If Christ be not risen, then is our preaching vain, and your faith is also vain." Can you think of a finer or fitter form of words with which to introduce your message than this smiting sentence from the pen of G. R. Beasley Murray: "Clearly, if Christ is alive, the world is mistaken"? Or maybe you are planning an address on the cleansing properties of the blood of Christ, and the text you select is I John 1:7: "If we walk in the light, as he is in the light, we have fellowship one with another, and the blood of Jesus Christ his Son cleanseth us from all sin." You would find it difficult to discover a more arresting mode of opening than by citing this striking and incisive remark of D. L. Moody's: "The most solemn truth of the Gospel is that the only thing Christ left down here was His blood." So you may begin with a quotation.

Pass forward now to the development of your theme, the elaboration of the points and the articulation of the joints of your sermon. You will notice that I am taking it for granted that there *will be* a development: a detailed, systematic threshing out of the thought implicit in your headings. Some men seem to suppose that, after they have fixed on the heads of their discourses, all they require to do is what farmers do with the heads of scarecrows—stuff them with straw! No error could be more fatal to the total effect of the effort. A piquant comment of Spurgeon's supplies a necessary corrective to this egregious notion. "To divide a sermon well," he says, "may be a useful art, but how if there is nothing to divide? A mere division-maker is like an excellent carver with an empty dish before him." See that you have always something substantial to carve. Remember that the divisions exist for the sake of the development and not the development for the sake of the divisions. Work out thoroughly, word by word, the material relevant to each section, set it forth in orderly array, and watch that there is no overlapping and that the transitions are made smoothly and logically, leaving no gaping hiatus between head and head. As to the order in which the divisions are to be arranged, place then in climacteric sequence. That is, unless chronological or other considerations commend the contrary, dispose them in accordance with their weight and import, passing from the weaker to the stronger and from the lower to the higher. If you do not follow this rule, the end will be not a climax but an anticlimax and your sermon, however good its beginning, will simply peter out.

From a discussion of the development of your discourse, let us go on to the debated subject of illustration. Having built up the walls of our homiletical house, we will now put in the windows. Some preachers indeed are too proud to express their thought in pictorial form. They deal in foggy abstractions and vague metaphysical formulas; their conceptions are generally cloudy and their messages smothered in theological cotton wool. You may *feel* what they mean; you never *see* what they mean. They are said by their admirers to be most suggestive and provocative preachers, but the only thing they suggest to some of us is a Scotch mist and we find them more provoking than provocative. They offer us hints and glimmerings and glimpses of the truth, but they never give us an open view of it. How gratifying it would be to their hearers if, now and then, they were to light up their meaning with a graphic illustration! It would be as if, amid volumes of swirling smoke, a brand were suddenly to burst into flame. Some men, to be sure, say that the thing is beyond them and that they cannot do it. "An illustration," confessed R. W. Dale, "is my despair." Others seem half-ashamed of their use of word pictures. Even John Wesley pruned all illustrative matter from his sermons before sending them to press. Surely that was a mistake. Doubtless, of course, it is only too tragically possible for a preacher to enter what Gossip playfully terms his "anecdotage," and certainly a sermon should always be infinitely more than a mere string of stories. Yet, handling such abstract and abstruse themes as you are obliged to grapple with as ministers of the Word, I do not see how you are to preach to average congregations with any purchase or to any purpose unless you preach pictorially.

Most of the popular preachers have done that. Spurgeon specializes in vivid and spirited anecdote. Guthrie's discourses are nearly all narrative. W. L. Watkinson illustrates his sermons profusely. Moreover, ought not the Master's example to be supremely regulative here? In seeking to woo the ear of the multitudes for his message, he made free and frequent use of living figures of speech. Metaphor, simile, analogy, parable, chastely and charmingly expressed, chase one another across the pages of the Gospels. Let it not be beneath your dignity to do what Jesus did. Make lavish use of whatever allusive and illustrative materials you can lay your pen to.

Occasionally, also, it may be parenthetically observed, a memorable illustration may be acted rather than spoken. J. H. Jowett, concerned in the pulpit one occasion to illustrate the difference between divine and human judgment, took up a Bible and a hymnbook and, holding the former flat, set the latter on its end upon it at right angles, thus vividly bringing out the truth that, while the world's division of humanity is always horizontal—lower, middle, and upper classes; lowbrow, highbrow, and so on—God's division is always vertical. Do not be above acting an illustration now and then, if you can do it naturally and without self-consciousness; but, if you cannot do it thus, better let it be.

Of what precise use are illustrations? To that question four replies may be given. First *they clarify*. That, to be sure, is their primary function. As we have already seen, they help to make plain what otherwise might be impenetrably obscure to ordinary minds.

Next, *they beautify*. The propriety of employing sermon illustrations for purely decorative purposes is indeed vehemently contested in some quarters. But surely ornamentation for its own sake is not incompatible with a serious intention, or else God stands convicted for the fashion in which he has framed the world. Again, *illustrations vivify*. They impart vigor and movement to the truth and cause thought to leap to life, as the motion-picture projector gives action and vital continuity to a series of still photographic negatives. Yet again, *illustrations verify*. It is perilous, of course, to try to prove a point by telling a tale, but surely a proposition in support of which analogies may be adduced from the realms of nature and of human life is, by and large, likelier to be true than one which does not admit of such illustrative corroboration. Illustrations are valuable in all these varied ways, and you will be very foolish if you do not try to utilize them in your preaching.

But the point is, where are you to procure them? An obvious answer is provided by encyclopedias of religious anecdote. There, any day, like little Jack Horner, you may put in your thumb and pull out a plum. Only the plums, by the time you come to serve them in your sermons, are apt to be very wrinkled prunes, devoid of bloom and juice, and people have a quite natural distaste for such homiletical dried fruit. Omnibus volumes of illustrations, in so far as they are valid pulpit aids at all, may prove of profit to you in the early years of your ministry, provided you use them chiefly as a mode of priming your own thought rather than as supplying you with ready-made chunks of sermon material. And, after all, the preacher who borrows an anecdote from such a manual must feel somewhat as does an angler when, having fished all night and taken nothing, he calls at the fishmonger's shop on his way home in the morning to spare himself the shame of an empty basket! Trout bought off the slab, however, never taste nearly as fresh as when you have hooked them yourself in the foaming river. Therefore, do your own angling! Cultivate what Sangster in a perfect phrase terms "a trawling eye." Look narrowly at life. Comb carefully the books you read. Study the newspaper. Listen to the tales people often tell in common talk. Each may have something serviceable to contribute to your fund of illustrative instances.

It is astounding how, to anyone with a homiletical mind, the homeliest happenings of everyday life may be conscripted for service as sermon illustrations. Incidents in themselves so seemingly trifling that you would scarcely credit them with possessing sufficient point or grip to win or hold the attention of a congregation can sometimes be used in this way with well-nigh incredible effectiveness. May I recount, as an example from my own experience, a simple story which, when preaching, I have more than once employed in striving to show how marvelously a sense of divine sonship and what it implies can thrill a man to the marrow of his being, causing him to rise superior to the most sordid circumstances and to triumph over frustration, defeatism, depression, and despair? Here it is:

Some years ago I awoke one murky November morning in our home in the heart of London. The weather matched the season. Fog was everywhere. It swirled up the river: it sprawled over the public buildings: it crawled up the streets: it crept into the houses—it even seeped into one's brain. I felt utterly melancholy and depressed. Life seemed drained of all delights, bleached of all color but a dull, drab gray. And then the postman came. I had not expected anything exciting in that morning's mail. So I picked up the letters with the casual languor of one who, in the expressive modern phrase, "could not care less." But then something happened. Among my correspondence was an envelope with an official appearance. On opening it I found that it was from the honorary secretary of the Clan Macpherson. Glancing at its contents, my eye fell on the following form of address: "Dear Fellow-clansman!" "Fellow-clansman!" The salutation acted on me like a charm. It instantly transported me, as if by magic, from that dismal scene. I was in London no longer. I was back among the Highland hills. I was hearing the pibroch sounding in the glen. I was watching the plaided warriors foregathering among the heather, seeing the gleam of tartan and the glint of steel. "Fellow-clansman!" My blood tingled at the thought. However drear my present surroundings, I was heir to a romantic tradition. Behind me there was all the color and chivalry and pageantry and splendor of a Highland heritage.

Often, too, you will find the newspaper a fruitful source of illustrative materials. I picked up a paper some time ago and spotted a fascinating paragraph which has since stood me in good stead as an illustration in a sermon on Isa. 43:25: "I, even I, am he that blotteth out thy transgressions for mine own sake, and will not remember thy sins." The illustration is as follows:

Not long since, I read in the newspapers about an exciting new scientific invention with which experiments are now being made in Australia. It is a radio-controlled flying wing, fitted with capacious tanks, from which, when the machine is in flight, large quantities of specially prepared chemical fluid can be sprayed on clouds as the plane passes through them. In this way, it is claimed, the clouds are dissolved and the sky may be kept perfectly clear for as long as is desired over an area of roughly a hundred square miles. The future possibilities opened up by this amazing human achievement are intriguing to the imagination. It is marvelous to think that man is now able to blot out the clouds. But why should we wonder at that? God has been doing it for thousands of years.

Sometimes, likewise, when browsing in the byways of biographical literature, you may light upon a vivid little episode which will lay hold of your imagination and illuminate for you some aspect of truth or experience or duty. Take this, for instance, from the life of James Kidd, of Aberdeen, the old preacher to whom I have more than once referred. You may use the anecdote some time in seeking to persuade your people to sit loose to the things of the world and to dwell much in thought on the glories of eternity. The incident occurred at a time when Kidd was moving to a new manse. His family had vacated the old house and the furniture had been removed. But, when the hour came for him to go, he could not tear himself away. In meditative and sentimental mood he paced the floors of the apartments in which he had lived so long. Here was the chamber in which his children had been born; there, the room in which he had studied and wrestled with God. Into his heart came crowding a host of hallowed recollections. Just then, however, his reverie was broken into by the entry of Betty, the servant girl. "Come away, sir," she pleaded, "come away. The time's up, and the other house is far better than this!"

As to the number of illustrations to be included in any one discourse, I should say that it depends very largely on the nature of the subject under discussion, some topics obviously requiring more pictorial treatment than others. As a general rule, however, never have more than three good illustrations in one sermon, one for each head, and see that the illustrations really do illustrate and not merely adumbrate the truth of which you are treating. Be watchful also of the wording of your illustrations. So much depends upon that. Not seldom a pulpit anecdote turns on a very small point and unless you are careful in presenting the facts, setting the details forth in proper order, and, especially where there is dialogue in the narrative, reporting the speeches with absolute accuracy, you may discover to your chagrin that you have actually bypassed the heart of your story and left the people vaguely wondering what you have been talking about. And the last state of a preacher in such a position is worse than the first.

Furthermore, vary the length of your illustrations in inverse ratio to the intelligence and interest of your audience. If your congregation is lively and expectant, you may sketch in your stories with a few swift strokes; but if it is lifeless and listless, you may need to loiter about a good bit in telling the tale, angling for the people's attention as a fisherman plays with a big salmon, and only bringing things to a brisk issue when you know that they have risen to your bait and got hooked on your barb. This is highly important. In illustrating their sermons, many inexperienced preachers fail altogether to land a catch because, as George Eliot whimsically put it, they do not sufficiently study the subjectivity of the fish. Summing up which subject, I would say that the question of the technique of effective sermon illustration is one which amply repays time spent upon it. Unquestionably, to tell a story well, with just the requisite number and the precise type of words to get it across to a particular company of persons and with such a disposition of its details and a paring of things to a point that it does exactly what you want it to do, no less, no more—is not that one of the most difficult arts in preaching, and one of the most rewarding?

Taking a step further, our thoughts turn for a little to the question of quotation. Should a preacher quote or should he not? That is a hotly controverted topic. Some reputable authorities are resolutely against it. Denney, for example, roundly declared that quotation was simply a lazy device to save a man the trouble of thinking a matter out for himself. It must be owned, moreover, that many of the greatest pulpit stylists do not quote. The sermons of F. W. Robertson are almost wholly bare of quotation. So also are those of John Henry Newman and Phillips Brooks. Other preachers, on the contrary, swinging to the opposite extreme, come out in their writings in a positive rash of quotation marks; so much so that, were you to strip them of their literary annexations, there would be precious little left to call their own. Here, again, therefore, it is wise to maintain the happy medium. For myself, I must confess that I am partial to a preacher who is humble enough to quote. However much I may appreciate and admire his own peculiar mode of expression, I find that after a time his style starts to pall on me and that I long for the relief, variety, and stimulus which studied and judicious quotation can impart to a discourse. Against the use of four types of quotation, however, I would especially warn you. First, those that have been employed so often that they have grown worn and threadbare. "Hackneyed quotations," as someone has said, "like the hackney cab, are outmoded and should be run off the road." Second, those that are so long and tortuous and involved that they break the continuity of your own work and seem like patches of bizarre material stuck crazily on to a background which they do not match. Third, avoid, for the most part, the use of Hebrew, Greek, and Latin quotations. For purposes of exposition, where a fine point is in dispute, this may sometimes be permissible, but generally it is to be deprecated. True scholars can usually contrive to express themselves in their mother tongue! And, in any case, people are not really so anxious as we commonly suppose to be reminded of the original—"reminded" is the courteous word though "informed" would be truer!—nor are they at all interested in the verbal quibbles which fascinate the pedantic type of mind. The matter is very much worse when such quotations from the ancient languages have no expository value, but are merely dragged in to give a dash of literary color or a whiff of learning to the preacher's style. Fourth, look out for what I may call "unconscious quotation," that unintentional plagiarism into which at times we are all liable to lapse. If you are not absolutely sure that a purple passage is your own, cut it out ruthlessly and cast it from you. It is better for you to enter into the pulpit maimed than with a wooden leg belonging to somebody else! With these provisos, I would recommend the practice of wise and tasteful quotation. Only, see that you quote accurately and honestly acknowledge your sources. Let your style be rich in happy borrowings and weave them well in. Notice how deftly the great preachers do that, grafting quotations livingly into their sermons with uncommon skill. Although they quote fairly freely, the effect is never that of a patchwork quilt, a medley of miscellaneous literary styles, or a mosaic of different people's ideas, but always that of a self-consistent whole—a seamless robe rather than a coat of many colors! I would beg you to make them your models in this matter. Learn how to quote from the masters of the art. Where are you to find quotations? A "trawling eye" will find them everywhere. Quote liberally, of course, from the Bible. "There is nothing," as Doddridge remarks, "that gives a style a more melodious and majestic cadence than Scriptures properly interwoven with it."

Quote, too, from the writers of the great devotional classics. Quote from general literature—though I would advise you to quote sparingly from fiction; truth is not only sometimes "stranger" than fiction, it is always "stronger" than fiction when used for homiletic purposes! Quote, in short, from any author who has something apt and apposite to say and who says it in such wise that, however you try, you cannot improve upon him: if you *can* improve upon him, do so; state the truth in your own way. Have a care, however, as I have said, to weave such quoted words or passages well into the web of your own work, and strive, on the other hand, to make your own style as worthy as possible of association with them, lest haply your sermon be in the end "like a mean dress bespangled with jewels."

As an example of the art of quotation at its best consider the following excerpt from a famous sermon by Alexander Whyte. Do you recall this passage of extraordinary power in his discourse on "Our Lord in the Garden"? Describing in that graphic way of his the arrest of Jesus in Gethsemane, he says:

> When the light of their lanterns shone on the dyed garments of the betrayed Man, who came to meet them, the Roman soldiers fell back. They had never before bound such a Prisoner as that. There is no sword-stroke that they can see upon Him; and yet His hands and His head and His beard are all full of blood. What a coat it was for which the soldiers cast their lots! It was without seam, but for all the nitre and soap they could wash it with, the blood of the Garden and the pillar was so marked upon it, that it would not come out of it. What became, I wonder, of that dyed garment and of that red apparel?
>
> If you have tears, prepare to shed them now.
> You all do know this mantle: I remember
> The first time Caesar ever put it on.
> . . . .
> Look, in this place ran Cassius' dagger through:
> See what a rent the envious Casca made:

> Through this the well-beloved Brutus stabbed,
> And, as he plucked his cursed steel away,
> Mark how the blood of Caesar followed it.
> . . . .
> then burst his mighty heart,
> And in his mantle muffling up his face,
> Even at the base of Pompey's statue,
> Which all the while ran blood, great Caesar fell.
> O, what a fall was there, my countrymen!
> . . . .
> Now let it work!

With these things said, let me insert a paragraph or two on the profoundly important matter of sermon endings. I am assuming that you *will* end! Some preachers appear to forget all about the homiletical full stop—"Amen." Others keep promising to close, but prolong the agony notwithstanding. It is well, in this connection, always to keep faith with your folk and never to irritate them through failing to be conclusive enough about your conclusion. Yet the finish of a sermon is a ticklish thing for the speaker. "In preaching a sermon," says Andrew Blackwood, "as in making an aeroplane flight, the chief test comes at the end." How best can a landing be made?

There are four approved methods. You may close with a peroration. "Do not leave off," observed Doddridge, "simply because you have nothing more to say: be sure to close handsomely." "Keep something of a canter for the avenue," counseled Denney. To be sure, the peroration is somewhat out of fashion at present. People are a bit suspicious of it, regarding it as a sort of homiletical last gasp, an artificially stimulated spurt or spasm, a rhetorical flourish that seems rather to call for a clapping of the hands than for a bowing of the knees. It is a discerning and justifiable criticism. All too easily it may become a mere feat of sermonic histrionics and, in any case, there is a great deal to be said for James S. Stewart's reverent contention that "diminuendo, not crescendo, ought to be the rule as we draw near the end." Among modes of sermon ending none is more artistically satisfying or spiritually effective than what has been beautifully called "the falling close." Yet I would not bar the peroration altogether. In the hands of a master like Spurgeon it could be used with terrific power. You may recollect the account of how, preaching once in London to a colossal crowd on "The Name of Jesus," he, so to say, "whirled the sling" for a while, mounting oratorically from point to point towards a tumultuous climax and ending, before he sank down in utter exhaustion, with the thunderous shout: "Jesus! Jesus! Jesus! Let my name perish, but let His Name last for ever!" Truly a noble and a notable conclusion, but a man needs to be very unself-conscious and genuinely inspired to do that sort of thing well. Any attempt to work oneself up to it would only result in comedy.

Again, you may close with a recapitulation. There is much to commend this. It forms a useful summary of the message, a concentrated epitome of its central content! Not only am I in favor of giving one's points at the beginning of the sermon; I also wholeheartedly endorse the practice of going over them again, if need be, at the end. Notice I said "if need be." For I do not judge it necessary or desirable in every case, but only where the sermons happen to be of a highly argumentative and closely reasoned character. Yet I do most definitely believe that many discourses would benefit immeasurably in distinctness and decisiveness and, what is more, would be infinitely more rememberable—a by no means inconsiderable matter!—if only those who deliver them would be at pains to recapitulate their points at the close. Then they might be surer than they sometimes warrantably are that their labor has not been in vain in the Lord.

Once more, you may close with a quotation. This, likewise, is a type of termination that demands delicate treatment. You may, of course, end simply by citing your text, and that is easy enough. And often the bare repetition of the text in winding up an address is a capital way of bringing it to a crisp, clinching close. No other signing-off sentences could so admirably conclude the discoure. But when you purpose ending with a poetic passage—as you may sometimes do with superb effect—you must exercise the closest care. Make sure that it really is poetry and not just stodgy doggerel. Nothing sounds worse at the end of an address than the recitation of a wooden, wobbly verse uncertain of its "feet." Be sure it really is poetry and then be sure you quote it sensitively, rhythmically, movingly. Here, if anywhere, as I say, you need to know what you are about; but, provided you do, you may use this type of termination with force and finality.

One fashion of finishing yet abides our question. You may close with a practical application. This is probably the commonest mode of concluding and the most serviceable. Here you aim at no soaring flights of sacred oratory, no logical tidiness, no poetic elegance. Your purpose is severely practical—to bring things to a head, to pare things to a point; in other words, to persuade your people to open their beings to receive the everlasting Christ whom it is your business and privilege to convey. Congratulated once on a magnificent oration, Chalmers, somewhat hotly, brushed aside the intended compliment, "Yes, yes," he said "but what came of it?" The greatest thing that can come of any sermon is that it should be used by God to transmit to some heart the eternal Word, that into some soul it should carry the Burden of the Lord. All other possible effects are secondary to this. Give your hearers Christ and you will do them the highest service in the world.

One further technical point. How long should it take to prepare a sermon? Obviously it all depends on what you mean by the term "prepare." There are really two types of preparation—direct and indirect. J. H. Jowett once declared that an address which took ten minutes to deliver at a midday service had taken twenty years to prepare. Plainly he was thinking about indirect preparation—all his theological training, his homiletical study, his everyday experience. But I am not thinking of that. I am thinking rather of the time required for the composition of a particular sermon. And again in this matter there is a vast diversity of view. Hear, first, Philip Doddridge. "Compose as much of your sermon as you can at a sitting," he says. "It will not be difficult to dispatch your sermon in five or six hours." Or listen to Hugh Ross Mackintosh. Granted that a man has been several years in the ministry, he maintains, "no sermon ought to require more than eight working hours for its composition." Or attend to Sidney M. Berry. "Two days to a sermon" is his succinct summary of things. To be sure, the time taken up with the actual writing of the discourse will be shorter in inverse proportion to the amount of study and experience which have gone to its production. Provided the preacher is in good physical and mental health and that he has taken pains to invoke divine aid, he should not, in the ordinary run of things, take more than ten hours to commit his message to paper. If he does, he will need to smarten his pace; for, what with Monday as a holiday and Saturday devoted to sermonic recapitulation and spiritual exercises, not to speak of the hours mortgaged every day to pastoral visitation, business correspondence, committee meetings, public services, and the like, no minister can afford to give more time to the drawing up of one discourse. Anyhow, never grudge the hours spent in sermon preparation. They are rich in spiritual spoils. No work to which a man can dedicate his powers is so magnificently rewarding.

As a footnote may I add that, when you have finished writing your sermon, you will probably find it profitable to lay it aside for a day or two, if you can, and come back to it later with a freshly critical mind. Guthrie declares,

> After my discourse was written, I spent hours in correcting it; latterly, always for that purpose keeping a blank page on my manuscript opposite a written one, cutting out dry bits, giving point to dull ones, making clear any obscurity and narrative parts more graphic, throwing more pathos into appeals, and copying God in His works by adding the ornamental to the useful.

Doubtless Guthrie went too far in that direction; but, without repeating his mistake, you were wise to follow his example in subjecting your sermon to thorough and most painstaking revision. Remember the old adage that trifles make perfection but that perfection itself is no trifle. Touch up the painting before exposing it to public view. Vision is indeed vital in preaching, but, for the finest results, revision is also necessary. Seek vision, therefore, but don't neglect revision.

Chapter Four

THE ENCOUNTER

THERE IS A MINOR but very moving episode in the life of King George V which is laden with meaning for the preacher. It is a stirring and dramatic story. His Majesty was about to speak on the radio at the opening of an important British congress, and his words were being relayed to America. Just as the broadcast was about to begin, a vital electric cable suddenly snapped in a New York radio station, plunging the staff into panic. What was to be done? More than a million listeners in the United States had tuned in and were waiting for the king's voice. But it could not get through. The live link was severed and transmission impossible. To repair the breakdown would have taken at least twenty minutes and by that time the speech would have been lost. By what means was the interrupted contact to be restored and the relay effected? Harold Vivien, a junior mechanic employed on the premises, saw in a moment how the problem might be solved. Seizing the ends of the broken wire, he held them, grimly and gallantly, as the current conveying the royal message was transmitted. Electrical charges of some two hundred and fifty volts shook his body, convulsing him from head to foot and causing him considerable pain. But he did not relax his grasp. Resolutely, desperately, he clung to the cable till the people heard the king.

What a picture of the preacher in action!—gripping God on the one hand and the people on the other, and letting the living Word through! You will never preach as you ought to preach until you preach like that—in touch alike with Christ and with the congregation and conveying through your vitalized and vibrant personality the voice of the eternal King.

Look, for a little, at this double contact which, while delivering his sermon, the preacher must maintain, and let us consider its aspects in inverse order, taking first the less important.

You are, then, to *get to grips with the people*. You are not to speak in a vacuum, pouring out words into empty space: you are to preach in a particular social context, to a given company of persons. And if you are to address them intelligibly, interestingly, improvingly, and to minister to their moral need, you will have to be at pains to get to know them individually in their temptations and aspirations, their sins and regrets, their frustrations and achievements, their hates and loves, their sorrows and joys, their fears and hopes. Like Henry Ward Beecher, you will often have to put your books by and study men.

Nothing contributes more signally to success in the pulpit than the psychological reciprocity between preacher and listeners which results from the mutual interest and understanding born of such private, personal encounters. It is as if there were hundreds of tiny invisible threads between the heart of the speaker and those of his hearers, and these he can pull at will, moving the congregation when and as he pleases, in the manner of a showman controlling his puppets by manipulating the cords which connect them with his hand. But no one ever thus handled an audience who did not thoroughly understand human nature.

Preachers there have been, for sure, who seemed to owe little to this popular response in their presentation of the truth. Of Chalmers, for example, it has been said that his sermons would have suffered nothing in their delivery had they been preached, not to the crowded and excited assemblies who actually heard them, but in Westminster Abbey with the doors closed and nobody but the preacher inside! But then Chalmers *read* his sermons. Had he delivered them in any sense extempore, he would certainly have been dependent to some degree upon getting *en rapport with* the people.

Here, then, is a basic law of live preaching. You must get to grips with your hearers. You must be at pains to institute harmonious relations between them and yourself. You must see that they are on your wave length. Declares Dale,

> There are some ministers who think so much about their sermons that they never seem to think about their congregations. They have so intense an intellectual delight in the exposition and defence of religious truth, that they do not remember that their business is to teach, to impress, to convert the living men and women who listen to them.

It is at his peril that the preacher loses touch with his hearers, for they have it in their power either to make or to mar his message. "A supercilious or frigid people," as John Watson well says, "can chill the most fiery soul, while a hundred warm-hearted folk can make a plain man eloquent." "Many a good sermon of mine," complained Alexander Maclaren, "has been spoiled at the beginning, because I got my eyes on a wooden individual or a slightly supercilious one, and could not quite forget him." So dependent was Spurgeon upon this getting *en rapport* with his auditors that he declared that it made him positively miserable and quite put him off, when preaching, if even a blind man ceased to face in his direction. Every impromptu speaker can appreciate that. But, on the other hand, if a frigid congregation can freeze the blood in a preacher's soul, an eager expectant one can set it tingling. "It is great congregations," says J. D. Jones, in a suggestive half-truth, "that make great preachers." Looking down from the pulpit upon a sea of uplifted faces—keen, alert, waiting for the Word—how can a man help catching fire? Yes! and the true preacher will feel the same authentic thrill when speaking in Christ's name to the irreducible congregational minimum, "where two or three are gathered together"; and, if he has already given full proof of his ministry, they, in their turn, will hang upon his utterances with almost pathetic eagerness, as those who look for their Lord.

Not that the minister is to make popularity the measure of success in his work—what Chalmers contemptuously styled "the popularity of stare and pressure and animal heat." That were to apply a false standard and to aim at an inadequate effect. We ought never to forget that it is possible for preaching to be popular and yet to be absolutely barren of lasting spiritual results. You may recall that moving story of how Guthrie, on his way once to the vestry after delivering a highly pictorial oration, overheard one of the female members of his congregation remark "in raptures" to a companion—"What a charming sermon!" Whereupon, the great preacher paused and sighed and muttered to himself: "Alas, my preaching is a failure, if it can only *charm* and cannot *change!*" You may have heard, too, of a father of the ancient Church who, when a sermon of his was followed by prolonged cheering, burst into tears because he felt it had not gone deep enough. Such is ever the spirit of the true preacher. "Accustom yourselves," Doddridge counseled his students, "to rise gradually above the views of interest and human applause." Popular preaching is of little value unless it produces spiritual results.

Nor must we lose sight of the fact that preaching may be popular and yet not be pleasing to God. Thunders of acclamation on earth are quite compatible with an awful silence in heaven. This point is strikingly brought out by the story of how a bishop preached once before a large congregation and in the presence of Francis de Sales. To considerable learning and culture the preacher wedded a gift of glowing eloquence. In great billowing periods he flung off a discourse more remarkable for oratorical brilliance than for spiritual passion or moral power. At the end most of his hearers broke into loud applause. Not so Francis. He remained resolutely mute. His silence nettled the bishop and he ventured to inquire as to its cause. "How did you like the sermon?" he asked. Francis pointed upwards. "You pleased all but One," he said. What an indictment! How shoddy our showy preaching looks in the light of God's verdict upon it! "You pleased all but One." May that never be true of you or me! Preaching may be popular and yet not pleasing to God.

Still, on the other hand, for the preacher to pretend to be utterly unconcerned about the reactions of his hearers to his message would be an unworthy affectation. Such an affectation might be a cloak to cover bitter personal disappointment. Let no man affect to despise the masses when he finds to his chagrin that he cannot capture them. "Sour grapes" should never grow on the branches of the true Vine. Have not most of the mighty preachers of the past been "popular" preachers in the best meaning of that much-abused word? Whitefield, Wesley, Rowland Hill, Spurgeon, Guthrie, Beecher, Talmage—all had the ear of the multitudes. There is, therefore, nothing inherently iniquitous in ministerial popularity.

We are not all built on the same scale, though, nor are we all capable of operating within the same sphere. The opportunity which opens the door to great achievement for one man would close the coffin lid on another. "Some men," as Seneca finely put it, "like some pictures, are fitter for a corner than a full light." Let us learn wisely to work within the limits of our powers—without, however, accepting our limitations too lightly.

May I remind you of Joseph Parker's apt fable about the ambitious watch? It has particular relevance to preachers. Suspended by a gold chain from the neck of a fashionable lady as she passed in her carriage over Westminster Bridge, the watch glanced up and saw Big Ben in its stately steeple far above. "If only I were where that huge clock is," thought the little watch, "how proudly would I tell people the time." The wish, we are told, was granted. By means of a thread the watch was drawn up to the top of the tower. But, alas, the farther up it went, the smaller it appeared to those on the ground; until, reaching the highest point, it passed out of sight altogether, and so was of no use to anybody. The moral is, of course, contentment with one's present location and, so long as that goes hand in hand with a hard and unremitting struggle to increase one's capacity, it is surely sage advice.

Nevertheless, whether popular or not, whether ministering to the masses or husbanding a meager handful, no honest preacher will want to carry on with his work unless he is profoundly convinced of its worth. And its worth is to be assessed not in terms of the satisfaction it affords himself as a mode of self-expression but of what it is actually accomplishing in the lives of those to whom it is addressed. Richard Baxter had the right of it when he wrote: "I have never known a man worth anything in the ministry, who had not a desire bordering upon unhappiness to see the fruit of his labours." Short of such social consequences preaching is only a subtle form of self-indulgence. "We come down out of our studies," says Talmage, "where we have had a grand time with Archbishop Leighton or Jeremy Taylor, and the people come up out of their stores and shops and homes, and we have known too little of each other."

To remedy this the preacher requires to engage in pastoral visitation. As Chalmers said, the quickest way to a man's heart is generally through the door of his home. Pastoral visitation often seems a sheer waste of time; yet, in point of fact, no part of the preacher's duty yields more handsome returns. Meeting a former parishioner after a lapse of years, you will sometimes be surprised, and perhaps a little mortified, to discover that he makes no mention whatsoever of your sermons—those discourses which you thought immortal!—but remembers with gratitude that you called once on his sick wife or ailing child. As Theodore Cuyler memorably expressed it, the minister needs both lungs and legs. And the legs are nearly as important as the lungs!

There are some men, it appears, to whom pastoral visitation is a crucifixion of the flesh—let us hope that it may also prove a quickening of the spirit! They shrink from it as a snail shrinks into its shell when prodded with a stick. Rather than visit they are ready to do almost anything. In one of his published sermons G. Campbell Morgan has a revealing autobiographical aside in which he confesses:

> I don't think my friends would describe me as unsociable, but I cannot bear near me anybody who creates in me a feeling of restraint. I am slow to make friends, or to talk to strangers. What would suit me would be a house buried in the woods, a quick transit to a crowded church—and back to the woods.

Now prophetic isolationism is not antisocial, though it may seem unsocial. No man can render higher service to the community than by getting alone with God and with the truth, provided he is actuated by a sincere desire to impart what he thus learns to those who stand in need of it. But there is no necessity to become a ministerial recluse. Preachers who leave the people severely alone often find, unless they are exceptionally gifted, that ere long the people leave them severely alone, and that they come at last in their pulpits to bear a pathetic resemblance to the pelican in the wilderness.

To be sure, there are those who brazenly maintain that the thing is beyond them altogether. Jonathan Edwards, Alexander Maclaren, John Henry Jowett all blandly declared that they could not do it. Well, I cannot understand that. I can understand a man admitting that he cannot preach, for preaching is a faculty with facility in which all are not equally endowed. But I cannot understand a man saying he cannot visit. He has two legs, hasn't he, and a tongue in his head? What more does he want? For all that, the great men I have just mentioned shamelessly protested that it was too much for them. They were not, however, like the minister concerning whom one of the members of his congregation is said to have alleged that he had "foot-and-mouth disease"—didn't visit and couldn't preach! These men *could* preach! Still, they were mighty preachers not *because* they did not visit but *in spite of* it!

For the fact is, the minister who does not visit not only deprives the people of a branch of his ministry which might be much to their profit; he also impoverishes himself in two directions. First, how much he misses that might have been useful to him as material for his sermon—insights into human character, stories from real life that far surpass in popular appeal the imaginary tales which appear in books, morsels of homely wisdom and quaint philosophy from the lips of those who have meat to eat that the world knows not of! But he likewise impoverishes himself in another direction. He casts away, as it were, a key to the door of the prison in which his studious habits are inclined to immure him. Let it in all honesty be confessed; it is possible to become terribly self-centered in the ministry. The very nature of the occupation tends to turn a man willy-nilly into a hermit. Alone with God and with his books he must get if he is to be of any consequence in his calling, and yet that very solitariness may be his undoing. Pastoral visitation provides him with an outlet for his, often suppressed, social instincts and so saves him from the melancholy and depression into which a man is prone to fall when too much occupied with his own thoughts. Luther when thus in low spirit was wont to run out among his pigs. I counsel you in such circumstances to keep better company. Off you go and visit someone and see how the black mood vanishes like mist before the sun. Sometimes, however, the despondency is due not to overabsorption in study but to reflection on the poor "statistical returns" of one's preaching. Dwindling congregations can have a positively shattering effect on a minister's morale. As John McNeill put it, nobody takes well to preaching in a woodyard. If the popular preacher has his perils, the unpopular preacher has his perils also, and I am not sure which are the worse. Here, again, pastoral visitation is the answer to the problem. There is a choice bit of homely psychology which no minister can afford to forget: "When a dog is not noticed, he does not like it: but when a dog is after a fox, he does not care whether he is noticed or not." To be "after the *fox*" means, for one thing, to be "after the *folks*."

And there is no finer way of banishing one's feeling of frustration and personal inconsequence than by sharing other people's lives and helping bear their burdens. Besides, who knows but that, if you visit *them,* they may return the compliment and visit *you* in church next Sunday?

A word now on a very practical point. Should your congregation not be large enough to fill your place of worship—a state of affairs unhappily all too common today!—take what action you deem necessary to see that the people do not scatter themselves widespread about the building, as though they suspected one another of having smallpox and were scared of contracting it by contagion! That sort of thing is fatal to the best sermonic effect. Henry Ward Beecher indeed once declared that he could undertake to electrify the greatest congregation provided its members sat close to one another but put them all four feet apart and he was done for! Wherefore, whatever you do, see that the people get together. You will be astonished to discover what a difference it makes to the delivery of a message.

Assuming, then, that you have been at pains behind the scenes to get to know your people thoroughly and that you are now confronting them on the fateful day, are you ready to begin? No! For not only is it needful for you to get to grips with the congregation: it is still more necessary for you to get to grips with God.

Of the place of prayer in the preacher's private life I have spoken elsewhere. In the pulpit that intimately personal experience proves precious beyond price. It is the homiletical hinterland from whose snowy solitary heights the rivers of our public ministry are fed and without which we become as dry as a Highland burn in summer. Observes Leslie Weatherhead,

Preparation for the pulpit is of two kinds, intellectual and spiritual. The intellectual is not difficult. You can at least prepare beforehand something that you feel contains a message. The great task is to be so spiritually at your best that God can use you to get that message across. It is supremely important to be in the right mood.

In his diary of private devotions Andrew Bonar has a touching entry confessing to failure along that line: "Have been struck by noticing how often, and especially no later than yesterday, in going forth to preach, I was like one seeking his own entrance into the Holy Place and fellowship with God, not like one coming out from communion to speak with others." Thomas Shepard, Pilgrim Father and founder of Harvard University, who is said to have worked early in the week at his sermons and spent Saturday preparing himself, had some severe, almost savage, things to say about those who were slack in this particular. He declared,

> God will surely curse that minister who lumbers up and down the world all week, and then thinks to prepare for his pulpit by a hurried hour or two on Saturday night. God knows, Saturday night were little enough time in which to weep and pray and get his sinful soul into a fit frame for the approaching day.

When someone inquired of Henry Ward Beecher, then at the peak of his powers, as to what was his method of preparing his sermons, he replied, with a touch of exaggeration for emphasis, that he had largely given over preparing his sermons and had begun to prepare himself. The necessity for that cannot too strongly be stressed. It is fundamental to the fulfillment of the true function of the ministry.

Always preach consciously in the context of the Presence. Be like John Brown of Haddington, of whom even the skeptical philosopher David Hume averred: "Yon's the man for me: he preaches as if Jesus Christ were at his elbow." Or like Hugh Latimer concerning whom the following unforgettable story is told. Preaching once before Henry VIII, he was overheard to say to himself as he mounted the pulpit stairs: "Latimer! Latimer!

Latimer! You must take care what you say, for the great King Henry VIII is here!" Then for a moment he paused, and afterward most solemnly added: "Latimer! Latimer! Latimer! You must take care what you say, for the King of kings is here!" Or like John Henry Newman, of whose preaching Dean Church somewhere says that its unique and original and characteristic power lay largely in his extraordinary realization of that spiritual world of which he spoke and in his manifest habitual recollection of the nearness of the Most High. Such preaching is mightily moving. "The most reverend preacher that speaks as if he saw the face of God," remarks Richard Baxter, "doth more affect my heart, though with common words, than an irreverent man with the most exquisite preparations." Wherefore, when preaching, keep close to Christ.

That is not to advocate an indecent familiarity with the divine. Of Spurgeon it was said that "he seemed at home with God." There is all the difference in the world between that and what H. H. Farmer stingingly stigmatizes as "being pally with the Deity." This last is shocking in the extreme. It is not hard, however, to distinguish between the familiarity of intimacy and the familiarity of impudence; and while, as preachers, you should cultivate the first, the second you should utterly eschew. God Almighty has his friends, but no "pal," and only an unimaginative irreverence would so presume upon his condescension as to prostitute the holy privilege of communion with him. Be intimate with God, therefore, but not improperly familiar.

Nothing will invest you with such confidence in the pulpit as the consciousness that he is with you there. You will feel adequate to the occasion because of your reinforcing association with him. Here, I believe, lies the secret of true leadership in the services of the sanctuary.

There is, forsooth, a species of religious leadership which is simply the expression of uninhibited egoism. On the face of things it may appear marvelously effective. Things may get done: there may be a certain sleek efficiency in the running of the ecclesiastical machine: round the pivotal personality there may cluster a coterie of doting admirers, buzzing about like bees round a hive. But the whole thing is devoid of spiritual value. Never was the Church of Christ meant to be organized round any human beings, however brilliant and magnetic, and the man who allows himself thus to be lionized in the house of God, not to speak of the man who deliberately courts it, is a ministerial Lucifer whose downfall is certain. True spiritual leadership is totally different. It is not the assertion of a dominant will, the imposition of an imperious purpose, the mesmerism of an electric manhood: it is the surge of divine power through a personality selfless enough to permit its fullness unrestricted flow, a surge of power so terrific in its impact upon the congregation that, before it, every lofty imagination is brought low and every thought taken captive to the obedience of Christ.

In one of the great Continental art galleries there is a famous painting which represents Luther preaching in a vast cathedral to a huge throng. The peculiarity of the painting is that, although the Reformer is in the pulpit, manifestly in process of delivering his discourse, the eyes of the people are not directed toward him at all. They are focused elsewhere. And, as you approach the canvas closely, you suddenly perceive the reason for this. Among the shadows in one of the corners of the stately building stands an ethereal Figure—the Figure of the everlasting Christ—and it is on *him* that the gaze of the people is fastened. That is a picture of preaching at its best—the minister in the pulpit but the eyes of the multitude fixed upon Jesus. This can never be, however, unless the preacher deliberately *wills* it to be, for Christ will never snatch the reins of leadership in a service out of the minister's grasp. He will take charge of the proceedings only when requested to do so.

Never fear that in thus surrendering a service to the control of Christ things will get, as we say, "out of hand." That they should do so is indeed a contingency against which it is well ever to be on your guard. "We are prone to drift through a service," declared J. H. Jowett, "when we ought to steer." But with Christ at the helm there is no danger that matters will ever get out of hand. They may get out of *our* hands—and the sooner the better—but they will never get out of *his*. No one can handle a congregation as he can. Ask him to take over from you and you may be certain he will. "When about to preach," said Luther, "speak with God." "Master, help!" Rowland Hill would cry at the beginning or even in the middle of his sermon. "Lord, help me" was Moody's telegraphic plea before standing up in front of his titanic audiences. Thus were these great preachers wont consciously to relate themselves to Christ, in the act of preaching, and to beg him to take control of things. Is it any wonder they were so successful?

I should be false to experience, however, were I to smoke-screen the fact that hours come in the ministry when, as you rise to address a congregation, you are suddenly gripped by a desolating feeling that God has withdrawn himself from you. At such times the language of Ps. 22:1 takes on new and terrible meaning: "My God, my God, why hast thou forsaken me? why art thou so far from helping me, and *from the words of my roaring?*" Describing such an experience, Bunyan said in that graphic way of his that it was like trying to preach with a bag over your head. Every seasoned preacher knows something about that. To what is it to be traced? In so far as it is not due to neglect of the body, to inadequate mental preparation, or to lack of discipline in the preacher's prayer life, it is, I believe, God's method of humiliating us upon occasion before the people lest, on account of the abundance of revelations, we become exalted above measure; and also it has the salutary effect of making it clear to the congregation that the excellency of the power is of God and not of us. What are we to do under such conditions? The answer is suggested by the story of two well-known Welsh preachers who were once bidding each other good night on the eve of a day of special services and sermons. "Well," said one, "I hope we shall have the Master's face tomorrow." "Yes, indeed," came the reply, "so do I; but, if not, let us do our best to speak well of him behind his back!"

There, then, to return from this very significant eddy to the main stream of our thought, you stand in the pulpit on the day of the encounter. On the one hand, you are in electric touch with the people; and, on the other, you are in vibrant contact with God. Thus you are homiletically "alive." The broken links, if any, between your congregation and their Lord are healed and harmonized, and what had previously been a mere aggregation of miscellaneous individualities is fused into a living fellowship, waiting in breathless wonder for the Word of the King.

It goes without saying that this massive concentration on the social and spiritual aspects of pulpit preparation ought not to cause us to be wantonly careless concerning the more mechanical aspect of the work. On the contrary, it should make us all the more concerned lest, through some technical hitch on our part, the royal message fail to get through or be but faultily transmitted. To the technicalities of transmission we now turn.

In the matter of sermon delivery four possibilities confront you. You may choose whichever you prefer. First, you can speak extempore—that is, literally, "out of the time," "on the spur of the moment," as we say, pouring out your soul, after the fashion of Shelley's skylark, in "profuse strains of unpremeditated." Or, second, you can put the discourse down on paper, taking the manuscript into the pulpit with you and reading it word for word. Or, third, you can write out the sermon in full, memorize it, and recite it before the people from stem to stern. Or, lastly, you can write the sermon out completely, make a précis of it or thoroughly digest it in your mind, jot down texts, headings, illustrations, literary allusions, arming yourself in the pulpit with the notes as an aid to memory.

The first method has not much to commend it. Archbishop Whately, indeed, whimsically remarked that it reminded him of the reply of Quince in the play to the inquiry of Snug, the joiner, as to whether the lion's part were yet written: "You may do it extempore, for it is nothing but roaring!" Mark you: I can scarce credit that any sane man would ever attempt to preach extemporaneously, unless he were, as the common phrase has it, "caught on the fly," and had had no previous notification. It may be, too, that, if anyone could do the thing well, it would be the finest form of preaching, but it is not a practice of which experience approves. Coleridge carries us all with him, on that point at least, when, in his celebrated *Table-talk,* he says:

> No doubt preaching, in the proper sense of the word, is more effective than reading, and therefore I would not prohibit it, but leave a liberty to the clergyman who feels himself able to accomplish it. But, as things now are, I am quite sure I prefer going to church to a pastor who reads his discourse, for I never yet heard more than one preacher without book, who did not forget his argument in three minutes' time, and fall into vague and unprofitable declamation, and generally very coarse declamation too. These preachers never progress: they eddy round and round. Sterility of mind follows their ministry.

John Watson has the same poor opinion of this type of preaching. He calls such sermons not extempore but "ex-trumpery." We may, therefore, dismiss it out of hand as a mode of sermon delivery with which no sensible man will have anything to do.

For the second method, however, there is something to be said —that of reading the discourse verbatim. It prevents logical looseness and woolly wordiness; it keeps a preacher closely to the point; it makes for accuracy of statement and dignity of diction: above all, it releases him from the mental strain imposed by other modes of delivery. In the hands of a Thomas Chalmers or a John Henry Newman it could be used with thrilling effect. Think of Chalmers in his Glasgow pulpit, following the spidery handwriting of his script, line by line, with the index finger of one hand and sawing the air like a windmill with the other; and then think of Newman in St. Mary's, Oxford, an ethereal creature, passionless, statuesque, almost angelic, scarcely moving a muscle and yet holding his vast academic congregation in thrall by his verbal magic, by his moral realism, and by that breath of another world which seemed to blow about him. Surely it would be hard to conceive of a sharper contrast. Yet both achieved quite extraordinary effects by reading their discourses. Among distinguished modern exponents of this method may be mentioned the names of G. H. Morrison, J. H. Jowett, and J. D. Jones. But the technique can barely be recommended without reservation for general use. After all, to read is not really the same as to preach. And, in the majority of cases, it must be owned, a *read* sermon is a *dead* sermon. Spurgeon has a word for us here. "The best reading I ever heard," he contends, "has tasted of paper, and has stuck in my throat. I have not relished it, for my digestion is not good enough to dissolve foolscap." "Never be a paper preacher," exclaims Leifchild. Sometimes a light surprises the preacher as he speaks, but it would be surprising if the light visited him while he *reads* his discourse! For reading almost precludes the possibility of revelation, which is a pity, because some of the finest things a preacher says come to him on his feet. Doubtless the manuscript *is* a preventive of pulpit nervousness; but how if, as Paxton Hood suggests, in parting with his nervousness the preacher part with a vital element of his power? A slack bow speeds no arrow, an unstrung violin yields no music, and the minister who merely stands up in cold blood to read his discourse rarely reaches the heart. That method, too, therefore, we may wisely set aside.

Memorizing the discourse—the third method—also has its advantages. William Taylor of New York adopted it most successfully for ten years and reported that he had found it eminently satisfactory. What are its strong points? Well, for one thing, it permits the preacher a larger measure of freedom than is possible to one closely following a manuscript. For another thing, it delivers a man, when preaching, from the misery of what J. H. Jowett described as "groping for a word"—though he, of course, had the word up his sleeve all the time! For yet another thing, it imparts to the preacher a certain workmanlike efficiency which creates in the people the bracing impression that he knows what he is about. Yet, for all that, the practice is not to be encouraged. There is usually something patently, sometimes even blatantly, artificial about it. It smacks of the stage or of the concert platform rather than of the pulpit. Everyone can see that the fellow is reciting. As James Reid remarks: "To memorize a sermon and read it off the back of one's mind is like reading from a manuscript so far as the distraction of our grip on the people is concerned." Besides, experience serves to show that, in most cases and in the common run of the ministry, the strain imposed upon the memory by this method is more than a man can bear. Of Albert Barnes, author of the monumental *Notes on the New Testament,* it is told that, when preaching on great occasions, he was in the habit of taking his manuscript with him into the pulpit; whereupon he would spread it all out before him and—*preach from memory!* "Now," he would say, "I am safe!" Should you decide to adopt this technique, you would do well to take similar precautions.

There remains, then, but one method to be considered, that of setting the sermon down in full—that you will require to do, in any case, if you are to make any progress at all!—and preaching from notes. In practice this mode has commended itself to most men. On one side, it saves the preacher from the vagaries of extempore delivery: on the other, it frees him from the strait jacket of the manuscript which inhibits, where it does not actually prohibit, the liberty of prophesying. Foremost among those who have adopted and advocated this method was Alexander Maclaren. His technique, at least in his earlier years, was as follows: writing the sermon out in full, he later transcribed the introduction to a separate sheet of paper and got the words, as we say, by heart. Into the pulpit he took with him only a bare outline or prospectus and a short memorandum of the points he meant to make and of any illustrative matter he intended to include—epigrams whose effectiveness in the telling depended so much upon the precise phraseology employed, and quotations the accurate use of which was with him a point of honor. That was all. Beginning to preach, he repeated the opening paragraph by rote, and then, shaking himself more or less free of the notes, plunged headlong into his theme, trusting entirely to the Spirit of God to direct him as to how precisely he should clothe this thought.

Confessedly, the practice has its perils. Unless great care be taken, the thing can degenerate all too easily into what Halford E. Luccock hits off as "an elephant sermon"—large head and little tail! That would be disastrous, because it is vital that there should be not alone an adequate and orderly development but, still more imperatively, a clinching, climacteric close. Yet there is no need, in employing this technique, to fall into such a trap. Provided the preacher has been at pains to write out the script fully beforehand, working the matter well into his mind, the transition from the memorized exordium to the extemporaneous unfolding of the theme can, with cultivation, be made so smoothly that the listeners are conscious of no descent, either in thought or language. What the second part may lack in formal dignity and logical consecutiveness is more than compensated for by the force and directness of its approach. And, what is infinitely more important—a consideration so momentous, in fact, as, for me at any rate, to rule forever out of court every competing method—this is the sort of technique which the Holy Spirit can best use, in the case at least of the ordinary minister, for the transmission of the eternal Christ. For this reason I cordially recommend it in preference to all others. I am convinced that it is the mode of delivery most fitted to fulfill the high end for which preaching was divinely instituted.

A minor matter here calls for brief comment. How full should the notes be that are taken into the pulpit? So far as it is possible to pontificate on such a point, I should say that it all depends upon three things: first, the quality of the minister's memory; second, the degree of thoroughness with which he has mastered his materials; and, third, the character of the message itself, some subjects naturally requiring more detailed and documentary handling than others. Be careful, however, not to erect a Paper Curtain between yourself and the congregation (you may find it almost as impenetrable as the Iron Curtain!), and, whatever you do, do not let your notes quench the flame which first-hand contact with the truth kindles in your soul. May I remind you of that excellent story about an old Welsh preacher, accustomed to speak extempore with extraordinary power, who, being invited once to preach the annual sermon for the London Missionary Society, inquired of two trusted colleagues as to whether or not, for such an occasion, he ought to use notes? "Well," agreed one, "for such an occasion perhaps it would be better to do so; but let us, at any rate, have plenty of fire!"

"But," protested the other, "he cannot carry fire in paper."

"Never mind," came the witty retort, "the paper will do very well to light the fire with!" Remember: too much paper will put the fire out; only use as much as necessary to set it ablaze.

It may not be inappropriate to interject in this context some observations on the propriety or otherwise of preaching old sermons. In my view the practice is permissible on three conditions: one, that the discourse is such as to deserve repetition; two, that it is not so remote from the preacher's present experience as to have lost its power to grip and thrill him; and, three, that the thing be not done too often. Let me expand this a little. On the first of these provisos Theodore Cuyler has some pertinent and pungent remarks:

A poor juiceless sermon should never be preached the first time; but a nutritious, savoury discourse may be all the better on a second delivery. Dr. Addison Alexander preached his glorious sermon on "The Faithful Saying" until he wore out the manuscript; and Dr. Griffin repeated his elaborate discourse on "The Worth of the Soul" ninety times. He never wearied of it; nor did his audience either. His congregations changed constantly, and memories are leaky. A first-rate practical sermon ought to be repeated (with extempore improvements) about once in five years. Fewer sermons and richer should be a settled pastor's aim. Whitefield attained great finish and power by giving the same discourse over again through all his missionary tours.

D. L. Moody, for his part, as you may remember, blandly declared that he always preached a sermon better after the twentieth time, and John McNeill delivered with immense acceptance all over the world addresses which, as he said, he had first given to a small group of Edinburgh washerwomen. There, then, is the first condition. Let the sermon be worth repeating and it cannot be preached too often; but if it is not worth repeating, it were better not to preach it at all.

The second condition upon which it is permissible to preach an old sermon is that it shall not be so remote from the preacher's present experience as to have lost its power to grip and thrill him. This is critically important. John Watson justly argued that we grow out of our sermons as we grow out of our clothes; and if the discourse which you propose to repeat is now too tight for your expanding mind, do not try to put it on again, or it will seriously hamper your homiletical movements. At all events this much is clear: if a sermon does not move you, it will never move others through you. Joseph Parker was asked once if he ever preached an old sermon. "No," he replied with that sly wit of his, "but I have never hesitated to repeat a new one." To the same point was Alexander Maclaren's pronouncement that he could never preach an "old" sermon, as such: before he could repeat a discourse, it was necessary for him to revivify it in his own mind by hours of thought and prayer. "I must give it hot," he said.

The third condition upon which an old discourse may be judged deserving of repetition is that the thing be not done too often. You may recollect the hoary joke about the traveling preacher with "two dried tongues in his brief case"—a horrible travesty, that, of the Pentecostal gift! Do not become a sort of homiletical hurdy-gurdy with a monotonously limited repertoire. Never repeat an old sermon because you are too lazy to construct a new one: do so only when you honestly feel that the old is better, that it is living and fresh and relevant to the needs of the congregation before you. With these provisos, then, I would endorse the preaching of old sermons.

What about preaching the sermons of others? I have seen this actually recommended in a manual of pastoral theology. Yet surely the thing is ethically indefensible. Sometimes, indeed, I have fancied that I should like to hear an actor declaiming from memory the mighty sermons of Chalmers or Spurgeon or Bushnell, but that at best would be a mere theatrical performance unworthy of the Christian pulpit. Besides, unless a discourse has been hammered out in a man's own mental forge, it is apt to be a sort of Saul's armor that dwarfs its wearer and prevents the free exercise of his proper powers. Nevertheless, it is amazing how many thus lift the sermons of others and preach them as if they were their own. One recalls that laughable episode in the life of Thomas Guthrie when, after it was announced that he was to preach on a notable occasion in Belfast, he simultaneously received six urgent letters from ministers in Ulster, begging him not to use a particular discourse of his, as they had anticipated him in delivering it in those parts! Moreover, there are certain "busy" preachers, it appears, who get their Sunday sermons regularly through the post for the price of a good meal: it is, however, at least doubtful whether the said sermons supply a good spiritual repast for their luckless listeners. I beseech you, offer no meat to your hungry hearers but that which you have brought down with your own bow and roasted on your own fire. Every preacher should be able to claim for his sermons what the street artist—sometimes with unnecessary insistence!—claims for his pavement crayonings: "All my own work"!

Hearing the sermons of others is a different matter. This is a habit it would assuredly be in your own best interests to cultivate.

I maintain that every minister should be, like the famous Tillotson of Cambridge, "a very attentive hearer of sermons." Listen to as many sermons as you can—good, bad, and indifferent. For, after all, if the fellow cannot show you how to preach, he can at any rate show you how *not* to preach, and that is always something gained. And, as you listen, be on the alert. Observe carefully alike the performance of the preacher and the response of the congregation; notice how the one evokes the other; and draw deductions therefrom which will stand you in good stead in days to come. "Take brief notes of the sermons you hear," Doddridge told his students. "Review them in your retirement. Transcribe them, and add memorandums of your own thoughts and reflections upon them, as you go along." You will never be a good preacher unless you are a good hearer. So listen to as many sermons as you can.

From these digressions let me bring the spotlight back on to the pulpit, where we will imagine you standing with your manuscript or notes open before you. Before you begin to preach, there are certain duties whose discharge is incumbent upon you.

To begin with, there is the great task of pulpit prayer. The importance of this part of the conduct of public worship it would be impossible to exaggerate. Yet how many able preachers fail just here. They find it easier to preach than to pray. James Kidd of Aberdeen once confessed to it. "I failed in this service," he admitted in his private diary, "most in my prayers, which smote me to the heart. It is a bad symptom of a preacher, who cannot address the Lord with fervent and suitable supplication." The words are well chosen. It is indeed "a bad symptom" of a preacher if he cannot pray in public; for the freedom and spontaneity and expansiveness of spirit which he experiences when addressing God in the pulpit will be exactly proportionate to the reality and regularity and rigorousness of his private devotional life.

Here is a story to drive the point home. During World War II a soldier was caught one night creeping back to his quarters from a wood close by, which was officially out of bounds. Haled before his commanding officer, he was told that a very grave view was being taken of the offense he had committed, and that he was being charged with holding communications with the enemy. The soldier protested his innocence and pleaded that he had only gone into the wood to pray. "Have you been in the habit of spending hours in private prayer?" growled the officer.

"Yes."

"Well, then, down on your knees, man, and pray now!"

Expecting instant death, the soldier knelt and poured out his soul in passionate entreaty. When he had done, "You may go," said the officer simply. "I believe your story. If you hadn't drilled often, you would not have shown up so well at the review!"

In your pulpit devotions you are to be on review and you will never do well there unless you have drilled and disciplined yourself behind the scenes. You cannot, of course, employ in the pulpit language which you would naturally use when alone with God. That is what Alexander Whyte meant when he somewhat cryptically declared that public prayer is an unnatural act. A certain reserve and delicacy and restraint are clearly called for in pulpit prayer which may be thrown off in private. And yet is it not wonderful how, before a vast congregation, a preacher who has been at pains to make God's acquaintance behind the scenes can open his inmost heart without shame and pour out his secret thoughts without embarrassment? On this head I would say two things to you: first, do not pray *at* people; pray *for* them. There is an oft-told tale about two men who went once to hear a famous preacher. He prefaced his sermon with a prayer more notable for flamboyant oratory and elocutionary effects than for spiritual intensity or moral earnestness. As the visitors came away, one remarked to the other: "Well, what did you think of the prayer?" To which his companion replied: "It was the finest prayer ever offered to a Boston congregation!" As likely as not, it was only the Boston congregation who heard it! "Prayer," as Spurgeon says, "must not be turned into an oblique sermon." Pray *for* the people, not *at* them. The second thing I would say is this: don't let your pulpit prayers be too long. God, as Oman said, is not a sort of Baal with whom his priests have to plead till the going down of the sun. Nor do the people, for their part, take too kindly to liturgical loquacity. They soon tire of a too-long litany. "He prayed me into a good frame of mind," George Whitefield observed of a certain preacher; "and if he had stopped there, it would have been very well; but he prayed me out of it again by keeping on." Don't let your pulpit prayers be too long.

And now may I add a sentence or two on the public reading of the Word? G. Campbell Morgan complains,

> I do not know anything that is worse done in the Church today than the reading of the Bible by preachers. That sounds very harsh, but I feel that it is so. There is a monotonous reading, and an academic reading, and sometimes a theatrical reading, which is just as objectionable as the rest.

We are all familiar with these various ways of reading aloud in church from the sacred volume. The monotonous reading is a dull, dreary drone, unrelieved by rhythm or inflection, a mode of intoning which reduces the whole thing to a lusterless dead level of sound; the academic reading is a sort of nervous nibbling at the Book's imperishable prose, the clipped, tripping enunciation of the pedant; and the theatrical reading is that which declaims the passage under review as an actor would recite a play, with simulated passion and dramatic elocution. Against all three you must ever be on your guard. To avoid the first, seek to modulate your voice: vary the tone to match the topic: import color and movement into your expression and bring out, as far as may be, the matchless music of the English. Be careful, of course, not to overdo it, or to put the stresses where they ought not to be, after the fashion of the uneducated preacher, who, thinking that the words printed in italics in the Authorized Version were intended to be emphasized, severely taxed the gravity of his listeners, in a public reading of the following sentence from the Bible, by loudly stressing the last word: "And he said unto his sons, Saddle me the ass; and they saddled *him*!" As an aid to effective pulpit reading you may find it profitable regularly to read the Scriptures aloud in your study; or, better still, out in the open and against the wind. Suit the sound to the sense and put light and shade, rise and fall, into your expression. Be specially watchful not to drop your voice as you approach the full stops. Take care of the consonants, and the vowels will take care of themselves. Practice speaking in the lower register. You will be surprised how such simple exercises, if persisted in for a while, will impart a rich timber to your voice and enable you in time to bring out the latent meaning of a scriptural paragraph or chapter by slight vocal manipulations. To avoid the second pitfall—that of reading pedantically—remember what Book it is whose words you are uttering. Of John P. Struthers it was said that in the pulpit he never read the Bible as if he had written it, but always as if listening for a Voice. Read it like that, and your performance may not be marked by elocutionary elegance or scholarly exactitude, but it will have something about it better far—an awing sense that from those holy pages sound forth the veritable accents of the eternal God. To avoid the third mistake—that of reading the Bible theatrically—it is not necessary to bleach your expression of all color and cadence and movement. You may never achieve the dramatic realism of the old Welsh preacher who is reported to have once read with such moving emphasis the concluding verses of the fourteenth chapter of John's Gospel that, when he came to the final words: "Arise, let us go hence," the congregation rose like one man in response to the command. Nor may you be able to vie in the impression produced by your public reading of the Bible with the noted American preacher who read the New Testament account of the Crucifixion so graphically that afterwards a member of the congregation declared:

When he read this passage of Scripture, we saw the faces of the Jews, with rage and cunning and hatred imprinted on them. I involuntarily clenched my hands as though about to assault the man who was insulting Christ. When he came to the prayer of Christ for His enemies, the audience actually sobbed aloud.

That, as the old Scots woman would have put it, was "fell reading." Probably, as I say, you will not be able to produce such powerful effects. It would be surprising if you could. Yet, if you are utterly sincere, you will never fail to warm the hearts of your hearers as you open up the Word of God.

Now let us pass to the delivery of the sermon itself. Once again, we will picture you in the pulpit. Your sermon, we will assume, has been fully written out and you would do well to see that, before attempting to give it, it is also well worked in, kneaded with the very dough of your thought. Of an old Glasgow minister it is told that he used neither manuscript nor notes of any kind in the pulpit, but wrote the heads of his sermons in shorthand on his fingernails. He had a habit of looking down intently at his hands when preaching, which led to the jest that he had his sermon at his finger ends! Evidently, in his opinion the best way to hit the nail on the head was to have the head on the nail! I do not propose that you do that, but I do urge you to master your sermon material before essaying to deliver it. And now, as you stand there, your personality poised between God and the people, vibrant with spiritual electricity and ready to convey the everlasting Word, you are in a way to embark upon your titantic task.

How do you start? You start, of course, by giving out your text, and I would beg you to make sure that every member of your auditory hears it plainly. Nothing could be more prejudicial to the effective presentation of a message than failure on the part of the preacher to let it be clearly known at the outset what passage of scripture he proposes to preach upon. Wherefore, give out your text audibly. Repeat it, if necessary, more than once. Utter it slowly, placing the verbal stresses where they ought to be. This is absolutely essential. People can hardly be expected to listen to your sermon with pleasure or profit if you cannot be bothered to tell them at the beginning on what biblical text or passage it is to be based.

That it is vital at the commencement to secure and to sustain the attention of the listeners is self-evident. As preachers, you must as part of your business, focus the consciousness of your congregation on one burning point of thought and hold it there, despite a thousand distractions, from beginning to end. This is by no means easy. Psychologists tell us that it takes a deliberate effort of the will for an average person to keep his mind for more than two minutes on any matter that does not grip him. Yet, if you cannot nail down the thought of your hearers for the duration of your discourse, you might as well not preach at all, for any practical effect your sermon is likely to have. As George Dawson once remarked to R. W. Dale: "When I speak, I make up my mind that the people shall listen to me. If they don't listen, it does not matter what you say." And Halford E. Luccock has a piquant sentence to the same intent: "There is not much use in holding to your subject, if you lose your audience." Now, in the pulpit you cannot *tell* people to listen or command attention, as can a schoolmaster in a classroom. The very attempt would itself be an admission of failure. You must *make* the people listen in spite of themselves. Your aim must be to secure what has been aptly termed "involuntary attention." If your hearers have consciously and deliberately to try to heed what you are saying, there is something wrong: they ought not to be able to help heeding you. It is, in truth, a ticklish task; but, says Paterson Smyth hearteningly, "you can make them listen, if you will pay the price."

Yes! but how? That is the question. By what means are you to evoke this involuntary attention? There are various expedients to which as preachers you may have recourse. One is to shout at the top of your voice, lassoing your people in a noose of noise.

You may have heard of the minister of whom folk said that, although they had often heard a better preacher, they had never heard a preacher better. The fellow roared so. "Scream no more" was Wesley's staccato counsel to one of his preachers. He who bellows unconsciously betrays the fact that he secretly fears that what he has to say is not worth listening to and that the congregation is in danger of discovering it. To shout is, therefore, unsuspectingly to display a subtle want of confidence in one's message. You may recall Thomas Guthrie's homely aphorism: "The drum is loud because it is hollow." Ultimately this attempt to secure attention by shouting for it defeats its own object. At the start it may seem quite successful. After all, people cannot very well go to sleep or divert their minds to other matters when a man is bellowing at them like a bull of Bashan! In the long run, however, the hearers grow habituated to the din and come to think no more of it than the lighthouse keeper's slumbering wife thinks of the foghorn which, but a few yards off, thunders all night.

Another expedient designed to exact heed from a listless congregation is the use of dramatic gesture. The sufferer in the pew, it is surmised, is likelier to pay persistent attention to what the preacher is saying, if the latter keeps signaling to him from the pulpit. Doubtless there is something in this, but the practice calls for skilled and prudent handling. Certainly it is not advisable to stand before the people with the stolid immobility of a tailor's dummy; yet neither, on the other hand, are wild gesticulations and frantic antics to be commended. The truth is that gesture, at its best, is generally unself-conscious, as when Coleridge, as a schoolboy, ambling along a street one day thinking of the story of Hero and Leander and fancying himself swimming the Hellespont, flung wide his arms as though breasting the waves. The moment the thing is done deliberately it tends to degenerate into a theatrical display. Gesture, when genuine, is usually due to the imaginative instinct of the preacher being suddenly stimulated into vivid action in the pulpit by some particular situation which he is describing: it is seldom premeditated or studied or self-aware.

On rare occasions it may yield remarkable results even when deliberately planned, but these are the exceptions rather than the rule. Take for example, the famous sermon by the old Welsh preacher John Elias on the feast of Belshazzar. This sermon was often preached with thrilling theatrical effects in the rural chapels of Wales. It was always preached after dark. Before delivering it, the preacher was wont to visit the places in which he proposed to give it, arranging for the candle, which formed the sole means of illumination, to be so disposed that, when he was preaching, his outstretched hand should cast a vivid shadow on the whitewashed wall, where all in the congregation could see it. Then, in the course of the sermon when the great moment arrived and the speaker portrayed the writing on the wall, the tension amid the hearers became terrific as, in bold silhouette, they saw the thing actually happening before their eyes. That, we are told, was repeated again and again and never failed to make a powerful impression. Yet it is more than doubtful whether it would produce any profound spiritual result.

Far otherwise is it when a preacher in the pulpit so utterly forgets himself as to throw himself bodily into his subject, employing illustrative physical movements quite unconsciously, and thus making his message live for his auditors as on any other conditions would have been impossible. Gesticulation comes more naturally to some men than to others; but when a man is truly possessed by his theme, it becomes instinctive for even the most undemonstrative to use the language of signs. Let me give you a few classic instances. Think, for one, of Krummacher, the great German preacher, describing in a sermon the scene in the dungeon where John the Baptist, kneeling at the feet of the executioner, was about to have his head sundered from his body; the preacher entered so fully in fancy into the situation and portrayed it with such graphic realism that, when he brought his right arm down sharply as if to deliver the fatal stroke, some of the ladies in the congregation shrieked and fainted away. Or think of Guthrie, preaching in Edinburgh on the story of David and Goliath, delineating the incident with such vividness and illustrating with such vigorous gestures the slinging of the stone that people in the gallery involuntarily ducked to avoid the flying missile. Or think of Philip Jones, Porthcawl, a picturesque figure of the old Welsh pulpit, painting for his people, with a wealth of colorful detail, the fruit with which Eve tempted Adam, and succeeding so well that some of the members of his congregation afterward declared that when, having described the forbidden "apple" with consummate skill, he swiftly raised the imaginary fruit to his lips and made as though to taste it, the very gesture caused their mouths to water! When a preacher, I say, can so forget himself in the portrayal of a scene as to produce that sort of reaction in his audience, he is certainly employing gesture to some purpose as a mode of gaining and gripping its attention. Far otherwise is it, however, when gesture is merely a wearisome repetition of meaningless muscular movements, a sort of clerical *tic douloureux*, like the spiral contortions of the preacher who shakes out his message as a horse shakes hay from its nose bag or the farcical antics of the fellow who, as Thomas Hood put it, is forever washing his hands in invisible water with soap that is not there! Such grotesque mannerisms, instead of helping to win heed for a man's message, actually tend to tell the other way—distracting the people's minds and ruining the effect of his discourse. Still, appropriate gesture, sparingly and unself-consciously used, can be of immense assistance to the preacher in the presentation of the truth.

But, indubitably, the best way to capture and to captivate a congregation is to catch fire in the pulpit. There is something fascinating about fire, and an audience finds a man aflame irresistible. Of James Denney it was said that sometimes when preaching on the great evangelical verities he would be "at white heat." Chalmers in action was described as "an incandescence." And once when Hugh Price Hughes was ablaze, delivering his soul on some subject that ignited it, a friend who happened to be near just then afterward declared that he dared not go too close to him at that moment for fear of getting burned! That is the way to preach if you want to hold the people and to get the Word across. Only it must be *real* fire; for, as Campbell Morgan has reminded us, "painted fire burns nobody"—not even the preacher! Get ablaze, then, and the world will turn out to see you burning. In which case you will use gestures in your preaching—fire has a well-known habit of flinging its red arms about!—but your gestures will always be the rhythmic movements of a body eager to aid its ardent spirit in the mediation of its mighty theme.

It may not be inopportune at this point to introduce the subject of humor in the pulpit. This is, of course, a vexed issue and one on which there is a sharp cleavage of opinion. Some would warmly contest its right to be there at all. The sacred desk, they would say, is no fit forum for the man who is trying to be funny. To make of the pulpit a platform for the display of one's wit is to debase it and to prostitute it to unholy ends. Now there is a good deal in that. Nothing is more odious than homiletical hilarity, and every right-thinking person has only contempt for "a clown in clericals." Moreover, when the Word is really on you to deliver, you do not feel in the least like jesting. It is the furthest thing from your thought. The seriousness of your purpose makes wit wither on your lips. Yet I would not ban it altogether. After all, it is good that even grave divines should show themselves human at times! And there is no better way of doing this than by, now and then, lighting up your sermon with a flash of humor. That the employment of such pleasantries in the pulpit is not incompatible with high intent and great achievement has been convincingly demonstrated in the ministries of such eminent preachers as Rowland Hill, Charles Haddon Spurgeon, John McNeill, and others. Few have had finer records as winners of souls, yet their sermons were very often spiced with piquant pinches of humor. Sometimes you will win people with wit where with pompous solemnity you would only leave them cold. But let me repeat: use humor sparingly and judiciously, lest with a joke you damn a soul.

Closely allied to the question of gesture in the pulpit is that of posture. This is perhaps a very minor matter; yet it does tend, more than we commonly realize, either to help or to hinder the work of the preacher. Is it not pathetic to see a man slouching about in the pulpit, or slumped ingloriously in a corner of it, as though his body were a gelatinous mass incapable of supporting its own weight, when he ought to be standing up straight—but not starchily so—before the people, combining in his deportment that engaging mixture of manliness and modesty which, as Robertson Nicoll believed, best recommends a minister to those who come to hear him? Posture must not, however, be confounded with mere pose. It is not a thing you can put on, as a man might don a mask: it is something rooted in the deep places of your inner life. A preacher whose whole soul when in the pulpit is, so to speak, at attention, taking the salute from the King of kings, cannot possibly appear before a congregation in a listless lackadaisical fashion unworthy of the dignity of his office and of the importance of his task.

Having, then, we will suppose, resolved that you are going to gain a hearing for your message, so far as in you lies, by paying due heed to the matters to which I have just referred, you will proceed with your discourse in a workmanlike way, always bearing in mind that your main business is not simply to utter a certain number of words but to give expression through your total personality to *the* Word.

Begin as slowly as you can, despite your racing pulses, reciting your memorized introduction distinctly and with deliberation, pausing after each sentence to make sure that the people are following you. Later, in the body of your sermon, they may be able to infer your meaning, where it is not quite clear, from the context; but at the commencement they have no such clue. It is necessary, therefore, to start steadily. You will accelerate automatically as you warm up, but at the beginning let your pace be that of the snail. You are to talk of eternity: so take time. Hammer the first paragraph home with punch and emphasis before you try to elaborate it in subsequent sections of your discourse. The old Welsh divines were masters of the leisured sermon opening. Here is a graphic description by Lloyd George of one of them launching out into deep water:

> It was like a ship getting out of harbour. The sermon had difficulty in breaking away. There would be an occasional bump, you could hear the chain creaking, but soon it came sailing out easily and smoothly on the fairway. Then you felt a speeding up and a slight heaving roll and you knew that you were being carried along into the open sea, the breeze filling the sails as you drove through the hurricane.

You may not be able to spend so much time as they did in merely crossing the bar: but, if you are wise, you will not unfurl too much canvas in putting out from the homiletical haven.

Your next duty will be to announce your divisions. The advisability of this is indeed disputed in some quarters; but, as I have already hinted, I am wholeheartedly in favor of intimating them as distinctly and decisively as may be. A word of wisdom on this matter comes from William Taylor of New York. "It is not the announcing of the heads," he says, "that makes a discourse heavy: it is the fact that, after they are announced, they are found to have no brains in them." Put plenty of brains into your heads and you need never fear to expose them for examination. After all, heads were made to be seen, and the more clearly yours are visible the better.

And now, leaving your memorized exordium behind, you plunge forward, like a swan breasting the waters of a still lake, into your extemporaneous development. As you speak, if you have a photographic memory—a faculty which can be cultivated to an extraordinary extent!—you will be able to see in your mind's eye the paragraphs of your sermon as you have set them down in manuscript; and you will be amazed how there, with the congregation in front of you, the Holy Spirit will bring all things to your remembrance, so that you will have power to recall almost the exact wording, without, however, taxing your brain as you would by deliberate memorizing. And, in this regard, may I advise you to train yourself to think paragraphically? Do not be content just to pour out your ideas piecemeal and in haphazard profusion. Visualize them in logical sequence and marshal them in proper order. Never forget that intelligent and interested listening depends very largely on this power of consecutive thinking and of consequent lucid expression on the part of the preacher. Of the style of John A. Hutton someone has spoken praising what he calls its "glorious irrelevancies." Make no mistake about it: most men's irrelevancies are the reverse of glorious. Wherefore, in your preaching keep to the main line: don't allow yourself to be shunted off on to sidings. After hearing a sermon by Rowland Hill, someone rudely remarked to the preacher himself: "You have taken us from Dan to Beersheba today. "Never mind," rejoined the witty divine; "it's all holy ground." Do not, however, permit the brilliance of the repartee to blind you to the folly of the practice. There can be no excuse for taking people from Dan to Beersheba when you ought to conduct them direct to Calvary. So stick to the point. Hold yourself rigidly to the matter in hand. It may help you to do this if you keep turning again and again to your text. Weave it well into the web of your discourse. Round off each head, on occasion, by reciting it. Use it also occasionally as a clinching close. In any case, reiterate it until everybody in your audience has it by heart. "Some brethren," says Spurgeon, "have done with their text as soon as they have read it." Do not be like that. Strike it over and over as the keynote of your address.

To warn you against certain common grammatical errors in preaching may seem like a work of supererogation. So perhaps it is; but, when you are speaking extempore, so far at least as your actual language is concerned, it is vitally important that you train yourselves to employ the English tongue correctly, as it were, by instinct, so that the proper usage comes naturally to you and you conform intuitively to the canons of good speech—not alone in the study where, with the manuscript before you, you have time to pause and consider, but also when on your feet in front of a congregation and ablaze in the delivery of your message. May I, at this point, offer you one or two crisp counsels? First, do not be so absorbed in the infinite that you split your infinitives; second, when using personal pronouns, beware of wrongly interchanging subjective and objective, saying "I" when it ought to be "me," and vice versa; and, third, if, in giving an illustration, you employ the historic present to heighten the dramatic intensity of the narrative, watch that you keep to the same tense till the tale is told.

Another practical point is the matter of pronunciation. And here we rub against the nettly issue of accents—local, provincial, and national—and the question as to whether a preacher ought proudly to seek to retain his native peculiarities of speech or whether he ought to try to get rid of them and to cultivate a professional mode of expression from which all such vocal idiosyncrasies have been sedulously eliminated. I think that in this regard a lot depends on where a man happens to be working. If he is among his own folk, his accent will quite likely be a help; whereas, if his ministry is being exercised elsewhere, the problem may be solved for him out of hand, his congregation being unable to follow him intelligently in the pulpit unless he drop his local lingo. Anyhow, nearly every locality has its own accentual irregularities, and some of these are so deep-rooted and so common in the neighborhoods concerned that if a man happen to hale from that vicinity he can hardly fail to lapse into them almost unconsciously. If, for instance, the preacher is a product of Scotland, let him have a sacred care not to transform his "r's" into "w's" or, worse still, into mere guttural grunts. Also, Rowland Hill once archly remarked that "h" was a small letter, but that he would have been "ill" all his life without it. If the preacher omit his "h's," it is usually the people who feel ill! So watch for vocal localisms.

While on the subject of pulpit speech, may I very briefly mention two things—the tone and the pace of your delivery. As to the tone, there is no need, as I have said, to shout, but it is imperative that you should be distinctly heard in the farthest corner of the church. It is told of Spurgeon that, when about to preach in a strange place on a great occasion, he would visit the building beforehand and test its acoustic properties. You may not have opportunity to do that; but, where you can, you should. If, however, you cannot do it, look very closely, during the opening part of the service, at the oldest person you can spot on the back pew. By examining his expression you will be able to tell whether or not he is catching what you say, and you will make any requisite vocal adjustments accordingly. In any case, be sure you are heard, or you might as well not preach at all. As to the pace of your delivery: I believe it is the almost universal tendency of inexperienced preachers, especially when under stress of strong emotion, to speak too fast. Even experienced, not to say expert, preachers have been known to do the same: of Phillips Brooks, for example, it was said that "his utterance was rapid almost to the point of incoherency." Now that is a pity, because often those who speak most speedily are best worth hearing, for the simple reason that they speak rapidly by virtue of the fact that they are conscious that they have something vital to say. Yet their pace is so swift that the majority of their hearers cannot fully follow them! Wherefore, let the spirit of the prophet be subject to the prophet and moderate the rate of your delivery so that none may miss your meaning.

Let me wind up with a few observations on the vexed question as to how lengthy a sermon should be. We are a long way now from the massive discourses of Puritan days, which were distinguished less perhaps for depth than for their "heavenly length."

Hugh Peters, a doughty preacher of those times, is said to have commended himself to Cromwell by holding forth solidly for three hours, inverting the sand-glass and addressing himself once more to the work with the bland remark: "Brethren, let us take another glass." It is highly doubtful whether any preacher of today would ingratiate himself with his hearers for the same reason. The tendency now is all the other way. And, within limits, the modern demand for short sermons is valid enough. Most listeners cannot concentrate on a sermon for as long as some preachers can preach one. "How long, O Lord, how long?" is the cry of many a modern martyr from beneath the perch of a loquacious pulpiteer. One sympathizes with the colleague of a garrulous preacher who, compelled to follow him once when he had been expatiating with great expansiveness on the excellences of his mother, observed with smiling satire: "I fear his good mother neglected one maternal duty: she never *shortened* him!" Some preachers could definitely do with shortening. Their sermons would be improved immeasurably in point and pungency if pared down to briefer proportions.

Nevertheless, the present-day plea for sermonic brevity must not be permitted to be pressed too far. There is a limit beyond which its claim ought not to be allowed. You cannot adequately deal with the great concerns of the soul in fifteen minutes. To permit one's discourse to be clipped and trimmed and truncated to such absurdly small dimensions is tantamount to admitting that the thing is not worth delivering at all. For, depend upon it: people will always find time to listen to anything which they judge to be important.

Still, after all, as Harry Jeffs aptly pointed out, the real question is not how long a sermon *is* but how long it *seems*. Ben Johnson in his *Discoveries* observes of Bacon as a public speaker that "the one fear of every man that heard him was, lest he should make an end." Evoke that fear in your hearers' hearts, when you are preaching, and you need never be afraid of being too long. To only a few, however, is it given to speak with such gripping gracefulness, and